A DAY WITHOUT A YESTERDAY

A Story Of Disaster – Tragedy – Triumph

By

Don Barrett

PublishAmerica
Baltimore

Hardcover 978-1-4512-7053-2
Softcover 978-1-4512-7052-5
PUBLISHED BY PUBLISHAMERICA, LLLP
www.publishamerica.com
Baltimore

Printed in the United States of America

Dedicated to:

Brenda Joyce
Shannon O'Keefe

Thank you for saving my life.

ACKNOWLEDGMENTS

The Editors and staff of Publish America.
The Board of Directors of the Metropolitan Homelessness Project
The Reverend Trey Hammond
Daniel Macke
Sam Carnes
Ken Jones
Sandi Hazlett
Bob Bowman
Pastor Cheri Lyon
Jim Summers
Dennis Plummer

The Staff of the Albuquerque Opportunity Center
Jessica Casey
David Cisneros

The Doctors and Staff of Healthcare for the Homeless
The Doctors and Staff of the University of New Mexico Hospital

The People who made my career possible:

Robert H. Goodman
Robert F. Lewine
Dick Clark

The People who helped me establish myself in Albuquerque
Brian Buckley
Ben Harrison
Liz Servis
Dr. Nels Dahlgren

A special thank you to
Dr. Susan V.L.G. Davis, PhD

PROLOGUE

There has never been a day like today, not in my life anyway. Oh there have been moments, events, periods of time that I hold close, locked forever in my memory, but nothing remotely like today. It was a day of days, a moment of moments, a fresh breath of life, the first morning of forever.

I have never felt like this before. It's not an emotion that I can categorize easily like love, hate, joy, ecstasy or anger. Although I've been accused more than once of being a word smith, there is no single word in my vocabulary to remotely describe the feelings running around inside me. Redemption comes to mind, but then I was never falsely accused of a felony, nor did I spend time in prison for something I didn't do, but that isn't exactly true, either. I was imprisoned, not by stone walls or the justice system, but by a reality I never knew existed.

We are all conditioned to believe there is but one reality, in which we live our lives, but in fact there are many. The world of the rich compared with that of the pauper is but one example. Neither experiences the other, they live in parallel un-touching worlds, much like the omniverse (an infinite number of universes ruled by different laws) that some theoreticians use to explain why intelligent life should exist at all.

Yet unforeseen circumstances can transport us through the Planck sized meniscus that separates one reality from another. I know, it happened to me. My reality now is different than it was only three years ago and to get to this place, I have passed quite literally through other existences. One day I was a family man with pretty much conventional values, the next a wandering vagabond, a ship without sails becalmed in hell, by doldrums of infinite duration.

If this sounds a bit metaphysical, it isn't. My story is not unique except to me. I am telling it so others will understand how easily the underpinnings of our lives can be torn asunder; how we can spin away, like a planet ripped from its orbit by a passing star, and most importantly how we can, in some cases, reclaim our lives from the vicissitudes of great misfortune, and in the end, triumph.

What happened to me was not a natural disaster. I've lived through three killer earthquakes in my life, one of which nearly destroyed my home, nor could you call it an act of God. Others, the victims of war or unspeakable crimes, have endured worse, but this happened right here, on a normal spring day, in the United States of America, the richest nation on Earth.

There was a saying popular some years ago. "Today is the first day of the rest of your life." I always thought it was a little too facile, but now having survived a certain kind of limited purgatory, I know it's true. This isn't about being "born again" or any kind of religious or spiritual experience, this is more like rising from the ruins of a rip in time, a life gone wrong and in the end – being alive and prevailing.

I am at least temporarily a survivor, but one who understands that the life we want to lead is never ours to own. It is lent to us day by day, hour by hour and only through adversity do we gain an understanding of what is precious and worth keeping as opposed to that which is base and can be discarded.

I don't want to spend too much time about my childhood, which just now appears to be a magical, almost mystical time, because it is relevant only in passing; but in order to understand where I am today, you must know from where I came. A chapter will suffice though it won't be as short as this prologue, however that doesn't mean as we proceed on our journey there won't be an occasional flash-back to some earlier point in my life. During my darkest hours my memories were the only light in the Universe.

This is a difficult story to tell and I do so not without some embarrassment, it's never easy to talk about monumental failure, but I must tell it if for no other reason than it could happen to you, and you need to know what I have learned at the expense of the person I used to be. So please, I ask you to stay with me, the journey is worth your time.

CHAPTER ONE
There's No Business Like Show Business

"Donnie, you're going to be a very successful man someday—a producer or, my God, a director."

That was my Aunt Yetta – I must have been five years old when I first heard it, and it was repeated again and again. Yetta was my Grandmother's sister. They were a comedy team, the Zwerling Zwilinge (The Zwerling Twins – though they were only sisters) in the New York theater just after the turn of the century; Yetta and Bessie were, quite possibly, two of the funniest women in the world, as I remember them. Grandma had to give up the theater when she married my Grandfather in 1909, but Yetta kept on going. She was a comedic star through the 30's when she made several motion pictures. In her hall was a life size picture taken of her when she was a swan, a fur stole draped over one shoulder, eastern European nose pointed well skyward. The picture paled next to her ego, which like all the other famous people in the family was enormous, no make that gigantic.

My Grandfather, Henry Scharf, was a "society" orchestra leader in New York city. He played the parties the moneyed swells threw for themselves and each other. His favorite venue was the original Waldorf-Astoria, which was located on what is now the site of the Empire State Building. During the summer season he toured the world on the great cruise ships which plied the Atlantic and Caribbean, leaving my Grandmother to her own devices, one of which was a thrillingly handsome Academy Award winning actor of considerable reputation.

Henry and Bessie's first born, Walter, inherited the family's musical gift (which I can trace back to 1835) and really began his career doing orchestrations for the George Gershwin musical, "Girl Crazy." In the mid 1930's he moved to Hollywood. His first assignment at Warner Brothers was orchestrating a song for a gifted but frazzled composer, who couldn't read music (a sin in my family). This melodic talent could only play on the black keys of the piano (the key of F Sharp major which is not orchestra friendly).

So, Walter's first break was setting to music the melody that came to be known as "White Christmas" for Irving Berlin. Not a bad way to start a film career, which included something over 350 motion pictures (the number changes depending on the source). That was my Uncle Walter, the man my mother expected me to emulate. He was her older brother and quite well loved and hated in the movie business.

As for my father, he had movie star looks, which I would have killed for, but no real concept of parental responsibility. He left on a business trip when I was two and didn't return until I was thirteen. My mother waited for five years, staring out the window as though she expected him to alight from a taxi, which never came. My Grandmother summed up her son-in-law with the expression, "feh dreck" (fooey shit). I've come to the conclusion that you can't put a curse on somebody, because I cursed him from the time I was five until I turned twenty and all he did was prosper, albeit in Atlanta and Miami, while I was in Los Angeles. Rich as he was, he couldn't find it in his desiccated heart to pay $75 per month child support so I did without a lot of things that my wealthier cousins took for granted.

The best part of my childhood was Sunday's at Uncle Walter's. Of course, I'm ignoring for the moment that he treated me like a note that was off key, sometimes known as a clinker. You see, he wanted his son to follow in his footsteps and become a film composer. Instead, Allen earned a Ph.D. in engineering and was in Mission Control when Apollo 11 landed on the moon. It broke the slowly hardening arteries of Walter's heart that his son was such a miserable failure as far as he was concerned. Add to that the annoyance that my mother was constantly pushing him to teach me composing and you can see why I was less than beloved unto him.

"Donald," he would say, "you have a lot to learn." God forbid you should have taught me something besides the meaning of misery and the feeling of being an unwanted presence.

Returning to Sunday's, we would board my Grandfather's boat-like Kaiser Manhattan (my Grandfather never owned a name brand car in his life) and cross the wilds of Laurel Canyon to visit Walter's multi-acre estate in the then pristine San Fernando Valley. There we would enter the baronial manor of Walter Scharf, replete with swimming pool, tennis court, basketball court, and a yard large enough to accommodate a game of professional football. It was simply spectacular, a testimonial to an ego as inflated as the Hindenburg by the hydrogen of success and fame.

Yet, it was the guests he entertained that made Sunday's so memorable. The man had made pictures with singers like Bing Crosby, Frank Sinatra, Elvis Presley, Barbra Streissand and Michael Jackson. I was too young to appreciate the moment, but I went swimming with Elvis when he still had a last name. Oh the teenage girls I could have had if only I had sneaked them in, but I was ten and not yet cognizant of the irresistible allure of fame. Basically, Presley was a very courteous man who refused to call my Uncle anything but Mr. Scharf and seemed like a nice enough guy, which was all he was to me.

I took swimming lessons with Diana Canova who was later to star in the TV sitcom "Soap" and played hit the bat with cousin Susan and Annette Funicello who was not so nice after she became a star on the Mickey Mouse Club. Donald O'Connor once danced for me and during the intermission of a Hollywood Bowl concert, Danny Kaye sang me his tongue twisting song, "Tchaikovsky" backstage, much to my Uncle's annoyance ("...why was I bothering Mr. Kay?" He asked.) It was a wonderful environment to be a kid. I was living in Show Show, the nice side of the industry, only later did I come to understand why they called it Show Business.

According to my Grandfather, who by this time had become my surrogate father, the highest calling on the planet was neither doctor nor priest, or even President, but rather a creative artist, preferably a musician or composer.

He had taken a shot at composition and actually made the hit parade of 1919 with an addictive little ditty called "Make the Trombone Laugh." It's true, you can find a recording of him playing it on the internet, but beyond that brief fling with original composition he ensconced himself in OPM —other people's music). Whether it was as a conductor or later in the music department at Republic Studios, he became less of a creative artist and more of an administrator. He would remind you, however, that he supervised (I use the word in the loosest sense) musical compositions by Aaron Copland (The Red Pony), his cousin George Antheil (the bad boy of music) and his son, who would later refer to his father in print as a third class musician, as a way of saying thank you, to the man who taught him to play the piano, not to mention the difference between a sharp and a flat!

Some families are toxic, mine bordered on Ebola. There were feuds and jealousies that ran amok for years at a time. The clan was divided in two: The Scharfs and the Silvermans. Bert Silverman was Walter's highly underpaid manager whom he was constantly accusing of keeping two sets of books (highly doubtful). So you had to take up sides and me being a little rebellious, I liked the Silverman's giving my Uncle just another reason to consider me unfit as a relative.

One day, Aunt Yetta (a Silverman) told my Grandfather, "You start all the fires around here." I heard that line repeated to every Scharf between Los Angeles and Poukeepsie. For all the anger, bile and resentment that caused you would think she was accusing him of pyromania, instead of common instigation.

Then there was the time that Bert's wife Laura and my Grandmother didn't speak for two years, although neither of them could remember why. That didn't stop them from bad mouthing one another in English and Yiddish. My Grandmother was accused of being an "Alta Cocker" (literally an old woman with diarrhea), while Laura was simply a "Shtick Dreck" (a piece of shit) – and we considered ourselves polite society, what a joke.

The other great memory of my childhood that made it magical were the evenings I spent in the company of my Grandfather's two brothers Uncle

Billy and Uncle Jack. In the early fifties, Tuesday, Thursday and Friday nights were spent at their tiny bungalow on Hilldale Avenue. On Tuesday night we watched the Roller Derby and listened to the brothers fight about whether it was fixed or not. Uncle Jack was a bigoted man who was coincidentally a hero from World War I. (I remember him secretly opening up a locked drawer and showing me the medals he won at the Battle of the Argonne Forest). His fun was blasting the skaters especially a little guy named Ralph Valaderez, whom he insisted on calling Saladereez (racism wasn't particularly subtle in those days). Uncle Billy, on the other hand was a sweet guy, who met his former wife in Burlesque. When I innocently asked why they had parted, my Grandfather said, with a twinkle in his eye, that Willie wasn't man enough for her. Maybe not, but he would go out of his way to take my mother and me on drives up the coast, all the way to Oxnard, through the then under developed country that the Chumash Indians called Malibu; in his wheezing, dyspeptic baby-shit green Dodge which he reminded us again and again was equipped with hydromatic drive.

Thursday nights was wrestling and the androgynous hormones were flowing like the Amazon into the Atlantic. Oh how Uncle Jack hated Gorgeous George calling him a fairy, and worse, a Nancy, but then there was their favorite, a woman named hatpin Mary, who would sneak under the ring and stick the wrestlers with a 12" needle when they would fall to the canvas. The brothers laughed until the three of them wheezed. It was like sitting inside the bellows of a Wurlitzer Church Organ.

Finally, there was that most sacred of televised events, the Friday Night Fights. "Look sharp, be sharp, how are you fixed for blades?" the animated parrot who represented Gillette would sing out and then men with names like Whitey White, Blacky Black and Yama Bahama would beat each other senseless like people who really couldn't do anything else. There was no talk of fixed outcomes, although there were probably plenty of them. Uncle Jack would occasionally throw a right left combination at the screen, while Uncle Billy looked on amused. He once confided to me that Jack, who among other things was a secret smoker, was so near sighted he probably couldn't hit the side of Los Angeles City Hall, the building from which Superman swooped a little later in the decade.

If I could pick the single most memorable moment of my young life though it would have been a father's day celebration when I was about 14. That manly day was typically held at Uncle Walter's because he had the space to accommodate the entire extended family and probably considered himself to be the most important father in the clan. This was one of those rare times both sides of the family, the Scharfs and Silvermans came together in a completely celebratory mood, probably with the aid of a little schnaps.

After the usual exchange of gifts and intra familial conversations that seemed amazingly without rancor or bravado something very special happened. In the living room, my uncle had a baby grand piano, which I had rarely heard him play. There was considerable competition between him and his father, my grandfather, as to who was the better performing musician (there was absolutely no doubt who the superior composer might be, Walter won that hands down).

At any rate, Grandpa sidled over to the piano, sat himself on the bench like a justice of the Supreme Court and began hammering out Rhapsody in Blue. Both he and his son had known George Gershwin and the latter had worked for him; each had his own familiarity with the composition and didn't need the autographed copy of the music which somehow disappeared after my grandfather died. About five minutes into the piece Walter strode over to the piano and proclaimed, "No, no, Gershwin played it faster."

Technically he was right, but then Grandpa's fingers were in their 80's and not as nimble as they once had been. Walter sat on the edge of the piano bench and slid across pushing his father off. He then picked up the piece on the last note grandpa had played and began performing it at break neck speed, his fingers moving so fast they were scarcely visible. It was a bit like dueling banjos but on the ivories of the baby Steinway. When the famous romantic theme of the Rhapsody began, the old man pushed his son back off the bench with Walter actually falling onto the floor this time, and played it with such romantic gusto that the entire family was entranced; Aunt Betty shed a tear.

When the piano playing competition ended, Aunt Yetta rose and began singing her signature song, made extremely famous by the Andrew Sisters during World War Two, "Bei Mir Bist du Schoen." (To Me You Are Beautiful). She began it as a romantic ballad, which is what it was intended to be, but then she took up a jazzy swinging beat and danced around the room, picking on Uncle Billy to do a mean boogey-woogey (who knew Uncle Billy could dance – but most of the that generation of the family had hidden talents – kept secret, at least, to me). Wow, almost immediately everybody was up and dancing, the ages ranging from kids to the otherwise elderly.

Then Walter's wife, Betty, began to sing some numbers that she had done when she was a sister act in vaudeville with Alice Faye (yes, the gorgeous blonde movie star). She was singing and dancing, while the kids were having the time of our lives as each family member with any performing talent, did a song, a dance or a comedy routine. Aunt Yetta's version of Hamlet was simply hysterical (so nu, make up your mind already and to hell with the arrows and the slings). I realized then the depth and strength of my show business roots; I knew who I was, but not how I was going to fit in with all these family legends.

So, I was a child of fantasy, movie stars, a show family and most of all this new fangled thing called television. My first conscious memory was watching our tiny ten inch RCA with my grandmother. A little girl named Kathy Fiscus had fallen down an uncovered well. KTLA the great local video experiment of Klaus Landsberg stayed on the air for 27 hours straight covering the rescue. He even had the novel idea of dropping a microphone down the shaft to pick up any breathing. It might have been the first time a home audience would know the outcome of a story before the people on the scene. Alas, the rescue was unsuccessful, but the telecast is still fresh in my mind over 60 years later.

While movies and the stage were the warp and woof of my family, I wanted something to do with TV. In 1957, a Tonight Show producer came to my school and requested a group of students to dress up in costume for President's Day (then March 4th). I was selected to be Teddy Roosevelt and appeared not only on the Tonight Show but also on the Today Show as well, where a minor disaster occurred. Ricky Cohen, who was costumed as President Lincoln and I were to make two appearances on the early morning program. The first went off without a hitch. In between, the crew treated us to a cup of hot chocolate, and the steam loosened the spirit gum on my mustache.

On live national television, Teddy Roosevelt's facial hair gradually slipped off his lip and stuck on his chin to the howls of cast and crew in Los Angeles and New York not to mention however many millions of people in the audience watching over their morning cup of coffee. I was a TV star for just under five minutes. Little did I know that the medium of television - Fred Allen said they called it a medium because nothing was ever well done - would consume the better part of my adult life.

CHAPTER TWO
Before the Fall

My own career in show business is the subject of another book, one I still have to write. Suffice it for this tome, I worked for more than three decades in film, television and home video. I had the privilege of dealing with some of the nicest and most talented human beings on the face of the Earth as well as a few for whom wading through the waters of their souls would not get your feet wet. Along the way, I managed to cop a few awards my most precious of which was having one of my shows named the 6th Best Documentary Ever Made by the Editors of Entertainment Weekly.

In 1987 I met a breathtakingly beautiful redheaded lawyer by the name of Jackie Ackerman. She was a graduate of Dartmouth College and Harvard Law, extremely intelligent, well-spoken with an aggressive personality that I rather fancied. Indeed, once in a dispute over missing royalties, in which we caught a major studio with their creative accounting hands in the cookie jar, she simply out negotiated the CEO, who never knew what hit him. The man's somewhat shady way of doing business was not a secret in the Hollywood community, but I doubt anybody had ever called him on it to his face. I got the monies owed to me, but you can be sure my business relationship with that studio was never the same. That's okay, there were always others.

We were married on January 17, 1988 and honeymooned on the big island of Hawaii. When we returned we moved to Point Dume, a celebrity laden neighborhood in Malibu, California. Within shouting distance of our home, were the dwellings of Johnny Carson, Louis Gossett Jr., Julie Andrews,

Charlie Sheen, Gary Busey, Martin Sheen and Cher. I was used to celebrities from my childhood and my work, but I think it was a novelty to Jackie and certainly her mother, Marie.

I recall that when my daughter, Torrey, was a young child there was a Halloween Carnival at the local park. We were standing in line for the haunted house with my mother-in-law when she noticed that Olivia Newton-John was standing behind us. My life experience had taught me that if you treat celebrities like they're your neighbor as opposed to someone famous, it makes them feel comfortable and you can have an enjoyable conversation or if they prefer, a respectful silence.

I merely smiled at Ms. Newton-John but my mother-in-law decided to ask me in an incredibly loud voice.

"That's Olivia Newton-John! She's a lesbian isn't she?"

I recall wanting to dig a hole to the center of the Earth and loose myself in the fires below. I looked at Olivia and simply mouthed the words, "I'm so sorry."

This little anecdote depicts perfectly how I felt about my wife's mother. We never got along, and I'm quite sure she hated my guts, although why someone should loathe another's intestines is still a mystery to me.

Long before the tragic events of September 11, 2001, the local joke was that with the fires, earthquakes, mudslides, civil insurrections and other disasters hitting Malibu our telephone area code should be 911.

Here we are living the great life, or at least the good life, Jackie is pregnant with our daughter, the date is January 17, 1991 our wedding anniversary. Interestingly earth shaking events have since coincided with that date. The first was the beginning of the Gulf War. We were prepared that night to celebrate a business trip with a visit to Commander's Palace, a fabulous restaurant in New Orleans, where we were attending a television convention.

In the hall, booths were set up by distributors of syndicated programming, old network sitcoms, game shows and the like. They all had television sets in them on which they were planning to display their wares. Instead all the sets were tuned to CNN, which was covering the action in the Middle East. I'm told nobody sold much of anything at that convention, which meant for some of my colleagues January 17th was a date which will live in syndication infamy.

Fast forward three years to the day, and we are asleep beneath the vault of the Malibu Milky Way, when about 4:00 in the morning a fault under the San Fernando Valley, about 25 miles away, ruptured and the Earth didn't just move back and forth, but up and down as well. If you've ever been in a big earthquake you know there are two distinct motions. The first is a horrible shaking which starts out tolerable and then gets worse and worse. The trouble is you never know how bad it will get. This time it felt like we were in a Waring blender. The second motion feels like the ground below has turned to water and waves are passing under you. This motion is not unpleasant, except it simply worsens whatever damage you've already sustained.

In our case, the house went in one direction and the garage in another. The 1994 Northridge quake was particularly strange in that it hit some areas especially hard, while barely affecting others. Malibu took a bad shaking and though this was the third killer quake to hit Southern California in my lifetime, none of the others had done anything but scare the pants off me. Luckily we carried earthquake insurance, but it had a large deductable and our bank account took quite a shaking. Jackie thought it was a good excuse to remodel and if that made her happy then it meant some peace in the family, and we went on with our lives.

A little over two years later, some arcing power lines started a fire twenty miles away, on the other side of the Santa Monica mountains in Calabasas, and the hot, dry Santa Ana winds gusting to hurricane force, turned it into a firestorm. The 1996 Malibu fire consumed 13,000 acres and got to within 100 yards of the house. The beauty and charm of Point Dume now held a good deal of terror for us, it was time to move.

Jackie had some legal prospects in Las Vegas, and although my business was really in Los Angeles, I went along figuring I could commute if necessary. We settled in Summerlin, an outlying suburb, which reminded nobody of the neon forest that is the Las Vegas strip. Nice people, nice home except I was unhappy driving nearly 300 miles in order to ply my wares. I tried getting involved in producing some live shows in Vegas, including one which would have involved a live participation version of American Bandstand, but Las Vegas entertainment was changing. The hotels were bringing in variations of Cirque d'Soleil and while they were very entertaining, the staging and production of these shows was outside my scope of familiarity. Thus, ironically, there was no work for me, the child of a show biz family, in the reputed entertainment capital of the world. Hmmm, as a child my nickname was Captain Show-biz.

I beat my head against that wall for eleven years, trying to live in Las Vegas and work in Los Angeles. Untying that Gordian knot was taking a toll on me and our marriage. I felt I needed to be there for my daughter and didn't want to do to her what my father had done to me. By 2007 my life was consumed by a conflagration of unhappiness. Like tectonic plates that build up pressure for years and then suddenly snap, my world was about to be turned upside down. As 2007 dawned, life as I had known it was about to come to an end.

As Edgar Allen Poe once said "All that we see or seem is but a dream within a dream." How true.

CHAPTER THREE
"The Fire Came By"

I had just returned from a trip to Los Angeles. It was a warm spring day, but inside the house, it felt like winter at the Antarctic circle. As I entered and put down my bag, Jackie's mother snarled at me. How dare she curl her lip. I had saved her life by agreeing to take her in.

Her son, my brother-in-law, was a career criminal and in between incarcerations he spent his time terrorizing his mother. He'd drive past her house and throw a big rock through the sliding glass doors, and then promised to do worse if she didn't give him money. A thousand here, five thousand there, it all went to cocaine, crack, crank and stuff I didn't even know existed. So with my agreement we invited Marie in to live with us and from the first moment I believe she began a campaign to destroy my marriage. To understand why, it's helpful to know that Marie's life was one disappointment with men after another. Her husband, while a hell of a nice guy never made it as big in business as she wanted and her son wasn't fit to be in the presence of normal human beings.

On returning home after one particular trip, Jackie confronted me with the news, "You're having an affair and I know it."

"What affair?" I asked for in truth I was seeing no one despite the fact that the familiarity of our marriage had long since escaped into space like the moon's atmosphere.

21

"Rachael (my beloved cousin—a Silverman no less) told me you said you were having an affair."

"What I said to Rachael was: given the state of our marriage I ought to have an affair." But I never did. I was that one husband in five that never ever cheated on his wife.

Jackie's mother claimed to have proof, but she had claimed to be able to prove so many things she never did. Nothing I could say, though, would change Jackie's mind. I knew little of divorce law, and of course, being a lawyer she could put me through a major divorce without working up a sweat. Although she had no legal right to do so, she threw me out of the house. I spent the next night at a male friend's, trying to make some sense of it and the following morning sought legal advice.

Larry the Lawyer basically told me I was in a no win situation. Jackie could prosecute the case to the ends of the Earth, and it would cost me more than I had to defend myself. It was a contest of who could burn the most dollars and I had as much chance as a three legged horse in the Kentucky Derby. Realizing I had to survive, somehow, I caved to a rather perfidious settlement, which left me with little liquid assets and a burning desire to get out of town. Las Vegas had never been my oyster, it was more like a capsule of cyanide. The only positive thing I can say about the whole experience was that I never lost a cent gambling. That's a record that continues to this day. I have the perfect system. I don't gamble in the first place and believe it or not, it works.

I couldn't stay in Las Vegas, so I had two choices. Go back to Los Angeles and try to re-establish myself, or to move on to a city where the motion picture business was in its infancy and needed some experienced hands. After staying just one more night with my friend, I packed everything I could into one huge bag, and not wanting to spend any extra money, hiked 12 miles to Mc Carren International Airport. It was cold, it was dark, and I was scared.

From the airport I contacted a pair of old friends, I hadn't seen in years, who had retired to Albuquerque, New Mexico.

"Oh yes, you can stay with us. We'll be delighted to have you until you get re-established." They promised.

It sounded too good to be true and it was. I landed in a heavy snowstorm, which should have warned me that things wouldn't be easy; snowstorms never portend anything good unless you own a ski lift. The couple who opened their house to me until I got re-established decided after three days I had to go. What had I done to offend them? I was good company, one could say even entertaining, affable, but on the third day, the woman, let us call her Randi, explained she was still mourning for her mother, who had passed away several months ago and I was a distraction. A distraction to mourning, sounds oxymoronic, doesn't it.

I didn't know where to go or what to do. I had just started looking for work and I needed the use of their computer to be totally efficient about it. Randi's husband found me a flea bag motel, where you could pay $250 a week for a room, yet for even that princely sum they wouldn't provide you an extra pillow.

Every day I went through the phone book calling up companies that were doing television and film production, as well as a lot of other things. Eight weeks passed and I was running out of money for food, lodging, cleaning and transportation. Although I hadn't ridden a bus since high school, I quickly became an expert on the Albuquerque Public Transit system. Money was getting tight, so I grew a beard, died it white, and got to ride the bus at the reduced fair of a senior citizen.

Day after day, week after week, I was being turned down more times than a bed spread. I shaved off the beard to look younger and still couldn't find an appropriate job. The problem was production companies were bringing their creative team with them, leaving the local jobs for electricians, grips and gaffers.

Sunday night ten weeks later it dawned on me that I had only enough money left for one more week at the Continental Flea Bag. What would I do then? As next Saturday approached I felt a knot twisting and turning in my stomach, always my weakest point when things weren't going well. Inside I was the San Andreas fault, about to rupture, and I decided to end it all on my last night.

On every piece of paper I could find, I wrote long good-bye notes, the most wrenching of which was to my daughter. I even tried to leave a voice mail explaining how my situation had deteriorated, but my call was never returned. At midnight, I took the sharpest edge I had, a plastic picnic knife and tried to slash my wrists. I failed miserably. The only way I could keep from going on the streets was to call 911. The police arrived and acted as though I'd committed a murder. My only previous experience on the wrong side of the law was with a traffic ticket. The paramedic's soon arrived to take me down the first corridor of hell.

We went to the Emergency Hospital where I was interviewed by three or four doctors. Was I totally insane, or was this just a cry for help? I knew the answer, but with all their education and training, they didn't. It was decided to put me in a locked down facility that dealt with highly depressive and suicidal people. Although I had gotten over the idea of killing myself, they wanted to observe me for a week. The people were very nice, dedicated to helping the patients, most of whom were in a good deal more distress than I. During the week I was there, I attended a lot of group sessions, private sessions and watched plenty of television. I noticed the more seriously depressed patients seemed to prefer "Judge Judy" over "The Price is Right." Despite the administration of anti-anxiety medication, I felt fearful. Where was my life going next week? I soon found out as on the third day they provided me with a brochure for a homeless shelter and that pushed my fear factor over the edge. I didn't want to go into a shelter with all kinds of crazy homeless people, you know the kind that hang out on the street and beg for money, but I could remain at the halfway facility no longer. Halfway? To What? Halfway to hell!

On a night when the rain fell like daggers, they bussed me to a street corner and told me to wait for a van to pick me up. I spent the entire night, in the a downpour dying inside over and over again. Once I approached a car, but the moment the driver took a look at my soaking clothes, and tattered appearance he burned rubber to get away from the spot. Apparently some wires got crossed and the van was sent to another location. I have never felt so alone in my life, nor so frightened, cold and wet. Downtown Albuquerque is gang country, and the streets were filled with tattooed menaces. Sure I wanted to die, but not the way they would carve me up. I walked and walked until I found a building called The Albuquerque Rescue Mission. It was 5:00 in the morning and they wouldn't open for breakfast until 6:00. I was hungry with five dollars left in my pocket and no immediate prospects for making more. Nothing to do but wait and pray some psychopathic son of a bitch didn't feel like killing me for a picture of Lincoln.

CHAPTER FOUR
The Invisible Odyssey Begins

The sun was just poking its bright face above the Sandia Mountains as I waited among four disintegrating blocks of what must have been once nice homes reduced to rubble, for some project that had yet to be started. I'm still holding a decent looking suitcase which makes me a mark for every thief hiding in the shadows. They won't take the clothes off my back, but I'll loose everything else, especially my medication. Before the axe fell in Las Vegas, I had just renewed some Rx's for anti-depression, sleep, and chronic indigestion. There just had to be a drug addict out there somewhere who could find a way to get high on this stuff. I stood in front of the mission, trying to assume the look of a ghost, the last thing I wanted to attract was anybody's notice. I soon learned that was impossible.

The first person who approached me was a portly lady, carrying her earthly possessions in pillow case slung over her shoulder.

"You new here?" She asked.

"First day." I replied.

"Scary isn't it, but I've been on the streets for five years and you get used to it."

I smiled, I had no intention of getting used to it. Once I found a job, any kind of employment, I'd get an apartment and try to figure a way to get my

26

life together. Even as those thoughts went through my mind, I heard my cell phone beep three times. The battery had given up the ghost and there are no re-charging stations on the savage streets.

A line was forming awaiting the opening of the Mission. Homelessness is waiting in line, sometimes for hours, only to be told there is no longer any room, food, doctors, nurses, medication or other necessities. If it was a Friday, it meant a weekend of suffering, or perhaps I should say another level of suffering, for each minute in the street you feel the remaining days of your life dropping like petals from a flower. I was 60 years old and at that moment I had no expectations whatsoever of seeing my 61st birthday.

CHAPTER FIVE
"Billy"

I stood by the wrought iron doors to the Albuquerque Rescue Mission, half expecting to see the words "Arbeit Macht Frei" arcing above it, but as more and more hungry people approached and entered the line, I realized this was a place of succor, not horror. From behind, I heard a baritone voice, that was to become my first best friend on the street.

"Hey man, you look mighty hungry."

With the voice went a contagious smile that parsed a face which had seen and done more than I would in a hundred lifetimes.

"My name is Billy." I took to the name, remembering my long gone great Uncle Billy. This Billy was black, my uncle white, it made no difference to me.

"I'm pleased to meet you, Billy."

He looked quizzically at me. "First time?"

I dug my toe into the ground, "Uh yeah."

"Embarrassed?"

"I don't know what I feel." I replied awkwardly.

"That's good. This is no place for feelings. Only thing that counts on the streets is survival. You gotta place to sleep?"

"No, I'm just one day out of..."

"I don't want to know. We're all just one day out of somewhere."

He pointed a long black index finger at a crumbing Victorian mansion across the street.

"Might be a bed for you over there. Place called 'The Good Shepherd.' You a new timer, they'll give you seven days. All you got to do is pass an alcohol test."

That sounded like a cinch. I was never much of a drinker and it had been, what, three or four weeks. I started across the street, and Billy let out of laugh.

"It don't open 'til 6:00 tonight. You better stick with old Billy or you won't live that long."

Well, that was an encouraging thought, but it made perfect sense, Billy knew his way around the streets, and now the wrought iron gate was opening and men were filing up a staircase to wait in line for breakfast. We trudged along with the crowd, up the stairs, through a room that looked like it was set up for showing movies and slowly wound our way towards the dining hall.

"Movie theater?" I asked Billy.

"Not one like on the outside. This is a mission. So everything you see is Jesus this and Jesus that. Not that I got anything against the Lord."

"I see."

"Upstairs they got a day room that opens at two; big screen TV, but they'll only show The Hallmark Channel, 'cause they don't cuss. Grown men sit around watching "Little House on the Prairie" and "MASH," passing the time waiting for dinner."

We entered the dining hall and took a plate on which some very nice older men placed eggs, pancakes, bacon and lots of syrup.

"Coffee sir?" Asked the server.

I didn't expect that level of politeness. I suppose I'd seen too many prison movies. You know, Yada Yada Warden; Burt Lancaster - Brute Force.

We sat and ate our breakfast. Instead of men staring silently down at their food, I found them talking about their expectations for the day, and what kind of lunch would be served at Noon Day (a luncheon shelter at the Broadway Baptist Church).

"Be sure and go back for seconds." Billy said. "Ain't much food between here and lunch."

I took his advice.

CHAPTER SIX
The Sidewalk

That first day on the street, I didn't know what would occupy me. My life had always consisted of something to do; appointments, meetings, time set aside for writing, editing or the 5 ½ hour drive between Las Vegas and Los Angeles. Now I had no schedule and the people around me, for the most part, didn't live by the calendar. Nobody really cared if it were March or June, except that the spring brought high winds to the valley and by summer it started getting hotter, but as they say, it's a dry heat, at least until the monsoons hit.

The most dreaded season of the year for street people is winter with its snows and unbearably cold nights. They call Denver the mile high city, but Albuquerque or ABQ as the locals know it, has neighborhoods that top 7,000 feet. It is the highest major city in the United States, so take that Denver (Bronx Cheer). During the cold season ABQ opens the doors to an old prison, no longer deemed fit for law breakers, and admits a few homeless to sleep on cots in the cells. The psychological effect of being derelict and "imprisoned" is pretty devastating. They open at 8:00 and put you back on the streets at 4:00 AM, the coldest part of the darkness. Still on a given night, regardless of the weather or time of the year, 2,500 to 3,000 men, women and yes, children, have no safe, warm place to lay their heads. Think of it, wherever you live, that in the worst rainstorm or coldest blizzard there are people outside with virtually no protection, merely trying to survive the elements, to get through one more heartless stygian night.

From the mission it was a mile and a half walk to St. Martin's Day Shelter.

"Best not to walk by yourself," Billy advised. "Lots of mean people prey on the homeless like we're a bunch of sheep."

"Wolves," was all I could think to say.

"Wolves, gang members, crack heads, meth addicts, if they think you have anything of value they will take it, and maybe if they be in a bad mood, they'll take you too."

I had never been in this kind of dangerous environment before. I was merely a gosling in Gotham.

"Don't the police…"

Billy cut me off with a swipe at the air.
"Look guy, to the police you are an unsolvable problem they don't know how to deal with you. At least if you're dead, you're just another homeless pushing up daisies. That they can deal with, but if they take you in, do mounds of paperwork, then they got to feed you, and that comes out of the jail's budget. On the street – well, what are they going to do? Nothing, goddamn nothing."

We walked the rest of the way to St. Martin's in silence. Billy was teaching me the lessons of the streets. Tough lessons, a tough life, almost unlivable.

"Why do you think that a street person in Albuquerque has a shorter life than a mine worker in West Africa?" He asked rhetorically.

Well, at least my first priority would be to survive from day to day, one night to the next. The trouble was I hadn't a clue as to how I would do it.

Arriving at St. Martins I noticed a long line of people waiting out front.

"Freeway patrol," Billy observed. "Pays $50 for seven hours of work, cleaning trash off the side of I-25; these guys start lining up at 6 AM, miss breakfast, go hungry until dinner."

"So much for homeless people being lazy," I observed not so brilliantly.

Billy rubbed his index finger besides his ample nose. "It's like everything else. Some are just trying to score a little drug money to feed their habit; others want to buy their way off the streets. Regular companies aren't standing in line to hire the homeless. Fifty bucks looks pretty good, when all you got is fifty cents."

Unconsciously I reached into my right front pocket where I always kept my money. My fingers searched for the tacky cotton feel of the $5 bill that represented my net worth.

"Careful, guy," Billy said, "You don't know whose watching. Somebody might think you got a bankroll in that pocket, look to rip you off."

"What do you do for money, Billy?"

"Disability! Once a month, the state hits my debit card. So what am I doing on the streets? I've been asking myself the same question for a couple of years now." He laughed, "I guess I don't feel like I belong nowhere."

We stopped and I looked him straight in the eyes for a moment.

"Everybody belongs somewhere."

Billy just laughed again. "Look around you, do these people belong somewhere? There ain't much room for philosophy in the asshole of Albuquerque."

St. Martin's didn't open for another half hour so we killed time watching people. Some stayed in groups; others went off by themselves and stared into space. Almost everyone smoked. The stink of cheap Native cigarettes

33

was pervasive, making the inside of my nose twitch – all my allergies were coming back. It wasn't as if they didn't know smoking was shortening their lives, their attitude -given the quality of their existence just wasn't worth maintaining. Dead men don't get hungry.

Finally, there was yet another line, as we were slowly admitted into the shelter. There were four long tables where we could sit, a couple of make-shift offices where counselors dispensed information about non-existent employment, (although no one could blame St. Martin's for the state of the economy). People were lined up in front of a bunch of overwhelmed volunteers, trying to help find housing for those who had gone years without a home.

In the back of the four room shelter was a mail drop for men and women without a mailing address. When you consider it logically the entire system by which society deals with the homeless helps perpetuate homelessness. How do you get a job if you have no clean clothes in which to dress for an interview? What do you tell an HR worker when they ask for an address and phone number where you can be contacted if you have no "where"? Is there any kind of work, other than the lowest paying, least skilled wretched job on the planet that would accept a homeless, rootless individual, and without work, how does one come to afford a home, a room or the barest necessities of life, toothpaste for example. Toilet paper!

Billy introduced me around, the names and faces were a blur, but one older fellow named Chris seemed to take a genuine interest in me.

"You're new on the streets, aren't you?" He asked.

"As new as you can get."

"So what happened?"

"Bad divorce," I answered not wanting to go into the lurid details.

"She really fucked you over?" Chris sympathized.

"She was a hell of a lawyer."

That brought a laugh from everyone within hearing distance.

"He was married to a lawyer and she fucked him over." The crowd began to chant "married to a lawyer." I put my hands up to my head, I was exhausted and now the target of these losers, but what was I, a winner in this crapped out game of life? With all my background, my work, awards and education I was no better than the guy next to me whose face looked as pitted as a gravel driveway. In fact I was worse. I had a life and I let it slip away.

Billy put his hand on my shoulder; gave it a pat. "Don't mind them; you're just the new kid on the block. What about your family? Couldn't they have helped you?"

My family; over a period of nearly twenty years my wife did everything she could to alienate my family from me, they were simply not up to her standards, and whatever success I enjoyed caused a jealousy and envy factor that spread like the ripples in a pond of failures. Truth was by this time the show business end of my family, the people with whom I had the most in common were dead or dying. Their children, with one or two exceptions, had found their way onto the public dole, their specialty having children out of wedlock. I looked down on them and they knew it, hating me all the more. How do you turn for help to people you've considered beneath you? Their reality had never been mine; that we were even related by blood was a genetic accident as much as anything else.

No, they would have shut their eyes, closed the door in my face and had a good laugh. Hey, high falutin' Donald is just one of us. Just take your seat in the back of the trailer, boy. I was as welcomed in their lives as a wrong number, when you're expecting an important call.

As for my daughter, she wouldn't speak with me, not for a second. Well, not entirely true. Once in three years she called to tell me my dog had died. Oh the stories her mother and grandmother must have told her to ramp up the hatred she felt. I was alone, as wretched and unwanted as the people with whom I shared St. Martin's Day Shelter. They were a family with whom I shared a misery as unbounded as space and infinite as the Universe."

"Fight, fight, fight!" People were yelling just outside the front door.

"Come on," Billy urged, "this is liable to be the highlight of your day."

In what passed for a patio, two equally wretched men in ragged Vietnam era army jackets were circling one another. One had his right hand wrapped in white adhesive tape, probably covering an injury, but at the time I thought cynically, to give him a little more oomph with a right cross. The other fighter's right hand had a glint to it, which I realized was the small blade of a scout knife.

"What is about?" I whispered to Billy, who had joined the on-lookers rhythmically clapping and taunting "Go, man go, go man go."

Billy laughed, "Usually nothing or less than nothing."

Overhearing Billy's response, the fighter with the blade screamed, "That faggot stole my smokes, all I had. He's gotta get cut for this."

With that he took a wild swing at his opponent who ducked, but not low enough, the tip of the knife slashing a red welt across the man's forehead. The bloodied fighter reached up and felt the wetness, then looked at the blood trickling through his fingers.

"I'm bleeding, from the head. He's trying to kill me," he screamed.

He then threw himself at his armed adversary, hoping to knock the man to the ground and dislodge the knife. Both men went down, then suddenly, as though lifted by a sky hook, the bloodied fighter was on his feet and in the grasp of an stoic American Indian who must have stood 6 foot 5. The Native had a "T" shirt that said "Security" and it was obvious to me he could secure anything he wanted.

Throwing the bleeding man backwards, he reached down and grabbed the wrist of the knife wielder, who yowled in pain as the bone cracked with a sound that made nearly everyone in the crowd wince and more than a few smile.

36

"You're banned from the shelter for a year." The Indian said, now holding the man off the ground by the broken wrist. Putting his face up to the yelping man, he spit, and threw him to the ground. With every eye in the crowd following him, he picked up a mostly empty pack of Natives and gave them to the bleeding man.

"Fucking white man, ready to die for one, two, three cigarettes. You get outta here too, you're disgusting."

"But I didn't…" the man began to protest.

"Law of the Shelter, you don't go after no one. You're scrammed for a week. Now vamanos."

"Fight an armed man over three cigarettes?" I looked at Billy who just shook his head.

"When you got nothing, you got nothing to lose."

"Dylan. Highway 61 Revisited." I said, recounting the source of the quote.

"You sure are a strange guy." Billy answered without a hint of reproach.

The day dragged on with the speed of an ant crawling across the face of the moon. I still didn't know where I was going to sleep and the thought of laying my head on a piece of unknown sidewalk was quietly terrorizing me.

After a one mile march to the Broadway Baptist Church where volunteers were handing out box lunches, following an hour's wait in line, we trudged another half mile to the Albuquerque Rescue Mission where the day had started with Breakfast. Across the street in a building that resembled a fortress was The Good Shepherd, where I hoped to spend the evening.

Billy tried to allay my fears.

"They've got plenty of beds, they'll only keep you a week; as long as you follow the rules."

"What kind of rules?" I asked hesitatingly.

"The usual, no alcohol, no drugs, no bad language. Lights out at 9:30. They'll assign you a bed, and oh, you gotta take a shower as soon as your admitted. They want to be sure you're not bringing any crud off the street."

"I can deal with that." I said quietly, unused to being deloused.

"What you can't deal with is the streets. You wouldn't last ten days. Now let's go upstairs and watch fucking 'Little House on the Prairie'. I understand Laura finds a raccoon today. At 4:00 there'll be a bed raffle, a private little joke here at the Mission."

I scratched my head. "Bed raffle?"

"It's a kind of street torture. See, they have about 45 beds here, but most of them is taken up by the 'program'. Those are the folks who are ready to give their hearts and souls to Jesus. They have a place to sleep as long as they need one. But, the mission leaves four or five beds open to keep on good terms with the city. They raffle off those beds and the winners get a place to sleep after they attend a one hour church service and a two hour bible class."

"How many people join the raffle?" I figured with rules like those there would be few takers.

"Oh, it varies, 75-80, sometimes more if the weather is bad. Folks'll do anything to stay off the streets, and sleep on a nice soft bed."

"Sounds like they make you pay in religious fervor." I said quietly not wishing to be overheard – after all, I'm a Jew.

"That's their business here. Helping us bums is just a cover. They're here to save souls – the old fashioned come to meetin' way." Billy snorted. Perhaps this wasn't his idea of how a good Christian should act.

Sure enough, there was a raffle, and just in case there was no room at the inn across the street, I entered. Everyone wrote their name on a small piece of paper, then folded it, and into the fishbowl they went, little snowflakes in a glass bubble. An unflappable volunteer with an ancient acoustic guitar strapped around his neck announced there were four available beds – "and who is going to get lucky? Who, does the Lord want to sleep between some nice clean sheets this fine night?" He taunted.

Wouldn't you know it, the first name he calls is Jesus Montoya, or maybe the whole thing was fixed. All I know is he spent the next five minutes doing hallelujahs and hosannas over Mr. Montoya as though he were the second coming of Christ himself, while 75 others breathlessly waited for their name to be called. Who would be among the chosen and who would be a portion for the foxes that preyed on the homeless streets and under the freeway overpasses of downtown Albuquerque?

Neither my name nor Billy's was called. I still had a shot at the Good Shepherd and as it turned out so did Billy. He hadn't stayed there in more than a year and was once again, eligible for a one week stay. I was a newbie, and thus deemed more eligible, by what set of standards I didn't know.

The other men not among the chosen four wore their disappointment like tattered old suits. You could see the thoughts spinning in their heads. What could they dig up for tonight. Some, among the wealthier class of homeless had sleeping bags and bicycles. They would high tail it away from the danger of the city and find a secluded spot in the highlands to the east, less than an hour's worth of pedaling away. There in some clearing with only the stars for company, they'd find some rest; the others would sleep with one eye open; and stupid ignorant people would pass by and idly ask themselves tomorrow: "Why do these homeless tramps have to sleep in our parks during the day?"

CHAPTER SEVEN
The Meeting

At 5:00 the doors to the dining room swung open and the line which had begun to form half an hour earlier made its way in. Only this time instead of going directly to the food service counters we were directed to sit at the tables and remove our caps. A bearded man wearing a stained white apron and a cook's hat strode to the center of the room and began to speak.

"I suppose you're all here because you are hungry," he began obsequiously.

There was the expected murmur of ascent. Billy, who was sitting beside me whispered, "Hang on, guy, here it comes."

The cook cleared his throat. "You know, brothers and sisters," – for there were women and children, entire families awaiting their dinner, - "I was once exactly where you are today. I was a sinner. I did drugs, there was lust in my heart and in my soul, I consorted with whores, oh how I consorted (laughter). I begged for dollars on the street corner and used my plunder to buy co-caine, speed and other forbidden products. I was helpless and without hope; I was on the Starlight 666 Express straight to the gates of hell, but do you know what I did?"

From one side of the crowd came a resounding answer: "You let Jesus into your heart – now can we eat?!"

The crowd laughed, but the preacher was not amused.

"This is not a subject for mockery or levity. You are here because all these fine volunteers, who have made Jesus their Lord God and Savior, are cooking and serving this fine food for you."

His voice went up a full octave.

"…and you will not make fun of them, or blaspheme the Lord or there will be no dinner this evening. You will have to fill your bellies and slake your thirst with prayer alone."

I could scarcely hide my shock. This place was here to serve the poor and needy, but as Billy had said it was in business of saving souls. If they knew I was Jewish, would they even feed me, or would they declare me an unredeemable sinner bound straight for the devil's workshop, as I'd heard the preachers declare on those 1,000 watt radio stations, I'd listen to while driving through Northern Georgia, scouting locations for a TV show?

He went on and on while the clock crawled and unfed mouths watered, until finally he came to the point of his sermon.

"Now who'll stand up with me and say to the world that he has let Jesus Christ almighty into heart and soul?"

Nobody stirred.

"I can wait as long as you can."

Finally, two men stood, bringing a smile to the face of the preacher chef, who bade them to join him in a final prayer, which he intoned with the solemnity of an Elmer Gantry in a tent meeting.

Softly, a woman, in a wheel chair, parked at the end of our table, only a few hungry souls away from me, began to pray:

"Baruch ata adonai elohenu melach ha-olam. Hamotzee lechem mien ha-artez." (Blessed are thou oh Lord, our God, King of the Universe, who brings forth bread from the Earth).

41

"Listen, she's speaking in tongues." A man observed.

"Hebrew, she's blessing the meal." I said quietly, hoping there were no belligerent anti-Semites at the tables.

"Hebrew, the language of Jesus." The preacher proclaimed.

"Aramaic." Billy responded. "The Lord spoke Aramaic."

Not knowing what else to say, the preacher allowed that beginning with table one, we could approach the servers and gather our dinner. I looked at Billy quizzically.

In that quiet self assured manner of his Billy said with a world of sadness in his voice, "Lesson number one, I may be homeless, but I am not an ignorant man."

I couldn't answer; I felt ashamed of myself for thinking otherwise even for a moment.

CHAPTER EIGHT
Big Ray and the Good Shepherd

"My name is Ray," he said as we stood outside the ten foot iron doors leading to the Good Shepherd Overnight Shelter, across the street from the Rescue Mission. Ray was a big guy, at least six foot six, weighed probably close to 400 pounds. When I shook his hand, my fingers were lost inside his palm. This was definitely somebody I wanted on my side if a problem arose.

"I'm new here," he continued, "I heard a new guy stood a pretty good chance of getting in at the Good Shepherd."

"That's what they tell me. I'm new too," I answered.

"What brought you to the streets?" Ray asked me what I expected was the most personal question in this society of the homeless.

"Ran out of money; new to Albuquerque."

He shook his head knowingly. "I was in the Army, tried to re-enlist but I failed the physical. Isn't that a joke? I mean wouldn't you want me to be your buddy in a fight?"

"I sure would." I said cheerfully. This was one guy I didn't want to piss off. He could have squashed me like a bug.

"Darn Army. You'll notice I never swear. I'm not allowed to – I'm a Mormon."

"Well, Ray, the doctor that drew me out of the womb was a Mormon. Back in Las Vegas I had Mormon neighbors, they always seemed alright to me."

The big guy smiled and unhitched his backpack. He rummaged through what looked like folds of clothing and removed a tattered volume.

"Ever read the Book of Mormon?" he asked.

"Can't say that I have."

"You ought to try it sometime. I'll loan you mine whenever you want."

"Thanks Ray, I just may do that."

A referee's whistle blew and the door to the courtyard opened. About thirty men tramped inside. We were made to line up as two guys the size of Ford Expeditions walked down the line looking at each of us. I found myself half expecting them to ask us to open our mouths so they could check our teeth, but that never happened.

Instead a third guy, much shorter than the goons, probably the head of security walked in front of the line with an old wooden soda box, which he turned over and stepped on, adding a few more inches to his diminuative height.

"So here's the story." He began in a contra-tenor voice, "Ten of you are returning as part of your seven day stay with us. That leaves fifteen open beds. New guys have first dibs, then if you haven't been with us for a year, you get second priority. Anything's left we'll lottery. Any questions?"

Clearly he wasn't interested in questions, as he immediately began reading a list of names, apparently the men who were in the middle of their stays.

"…Baker, Gonzales, Porto Fuego, Weber, front and center."

The men called did as they were told. Another security type then came forward with a device that I had never seen before.

"Okay," he said to the first of the front-and centers, "blow into this."

I looked questioningly at Billy.

"Breathalyzer," he whispered to me. "They won't take you if you've been drinking."

Big Ray overheard, "No problem, we Mormons don't drink, not even Coca Cola – caffeine is forbidden."

I hadn't had a drink since coming to Albuquerque, so I knew I was clear, but what if the machine malfunctioned and they wouldn't let me in? I was counting on this as a place to stay. I couldn't survive on the streets. A knot the size of a Satsuma plum formed in my stomach. I suddenly realized how vulnerable I was; for the first time my condition of being without any nighttime shelter really hit me. This was no camping trip, it was survival as no TV reality show had ever depicted it.

"What about new guys?" The security guard blared.

I raised my hand and stepped forward aggressively. I couldn't afford to be turned down.

"What's your name?"

I gave him my name, straight forward no attitude.

"Okay blow into this."

I blew until I thought my lungs would explode. The guard holding the instrument watched intently as the needle failed to move a centimeter.

Nodded his head, "He's clean."

I was sent through a small door and into a large hall that served as an entry room and dining hall. Once again I waited in line, while a man in baggy shorts wearing a Buffalo Bills cap took down pertinent information about each "guest" who would be spending the night. Billy followed me in and once again had my back, then came Big Ray who almost hit his head on a naked cross beam that hung below the ceiling. We waited as each man in turn was questioned and briefly examined for open lesions or festering sores.

Once I had passed muster they gave me a towel and a box for any personal items.

"You're assigned bed 19 top bunk. Everybody takes a shower first. We don't want no bugs in our beds."

So I was no longer whom I had been, I was now a potential source of vermin and disease, one that had to be checked out and then thrust into a hot shower to be thoroughly cleaned.

"Make sure you wash you hair," yet another security guard told me as I entered the shower area. "Ten minutes, after that we turn off the hot water."

Following the shower, which I confess felt pretty good, I was given a pair of pajamas which would be laundered every day. Actually they were more like the scrubs that seem to be favored in hospitals, and I was in no position to complain.

I decided to reconnoiter the area, figuring I would run into Billy or Big Ray at some point. The first place I headed was the TV Room, or somebody's idea of a TV Room joke. In a 15 x 20 foot space, there was a card table on which sat a 14" television. There were no chairs and only two viewers, one of whom had the other in a head lock. This was undoubtedly not the place for me to be, since the two men were mimicking what they saw on a broadcast of the Ultimate Fighting Championship or Octagon or some such androgenic competition. Since I had no intention of submitting to a head lock, or any other kind of lock, I walked quickly into the next room. It was the library.

There I was unimpressed by at least 50 books in various states of disrepair, completely alone. Apparently, the library wasn't high on list, not like NBC, the place to be.

Curious, there must have been thirty or forty men on the premises, so far I'd found only two. Everybody had to be somewhere, I reasoned brilliantly, and continued through yet another door. This time I hit the jackpot. It was the pool hall or as the Good Shepherds would call it, the recreation room.

There was a single table and at least thirty men surrounding it, while two guys without much more than average street talent were squaring off in a game of eight ball. I was surprised to find that the crowd was betting heavily, albeit in cigarettes, on the player with an overhand bridge that looked like it was about to collapse into the Mississippi and take the cue with it. I learned his name was Snooker and he'd won four games in a row, over which twenty cartons of Natives had changed hands.

Having nothing to wager, I stood and watched as Snooker blew an easy shot that would have lined him up for the eight ball. Back in the day, I had a girlfriend in college whose dad had a prized Brunswick Willie Mosconi model pool table and knew how to use it. After tiring of watching his daughter run the table on me time after time, Seymour decided to give me a lesson or two. Before long I realized I had a feel for the geometry of the game, and along with Shari we would frequently take on other couples at the Student Union. Those matches paid for more than one expensive dinner.

I sidled up to Billy. "Uh, what does it take to play this guy?"

"At least two cartons—you know how to play pool?" Billy asked as though he thought pool was too rough and tumble for a tender ass like me.

"I can play a damn site better than this guy."

"You sure? Hmmm, let me do some manipulating."

Billy backed off into the crowd and for a moment, I figured he just didn't want any part of this action. Then he popped out again.

"Don't disappointment me, guy. I haven't exactly been on a roll."

When the game ended, Snooker happily looked around the crowd of winners who'd bet on him – he was going to get his cut - and disdainfully at losers who'd bet on anyone sucker enough to wager against him.

"Anymore losers want to take a chance against the Snook-ster?" He boasted

I slowly walked up to the table and slapped down two cartons of Virgin Natives.

"Lag for break?"

"Sure, why not?" Snooker said with an air of supreme confidence.

We both took our positions at the foot rail and simultaneously cued our chosen balls, rolling to the head rail at the far end of the table. Whoever could bounce his ball off the head rail and stop it closest to the foot rail would win the break and an instant advantage in the game. Snooker wasn't bad. His ball slowed as if it had a set of Girling hydraulic brakes attached and stopped about an inch and a half from the foot rail. Apparently, with all that had happened to me since leaving Las Vegas, my touch on the cue was as good as ever. My ball froze against the foot rail, you couldn't have slipped an ace of diamonds between ball and velvet, to the cheers of everyone but those who'd bet on the Snook-ster himself.

"Fucking lucky?" Was all he could manage. "Break's another thing." Oh my goodness, an F-bomb at the Good Shepherd.

One of the spectators who had made himself the referee, racked the balls in the wooden triangle with eight ball dead center.

"Gimme a nice tight rack," I said, playing with Snooker's head a little.

"You got it, tight as a virgin's twat," the ref responded with poetry that would have made Lord Byron nauseas.

I set myself with an eye on the ball just to the right of the closest or head ball in the triangle. Adding some chalk to the cue so it wouldn't slip off the side, I drew my right hand back and as smoothly as I could manage and drove the cue with a little left spin angle(English) into the right side of the head ball. The rack scattered so fast it was impossible to follow any particular ball. A clunk meant one had dropped and everyone in the crowd looked to see if it were a solid or a stripe.

"Goddamn, he sunk the eight ball." Someone cried out.

The crowd buzzed. "Game," I said, laying the cue on the table.

"What the fuck!" Snooker was either impressed or pissed off, I couldn't tell which, come to think of it he was a little of both.

"You gonna walk away or let me get even?" He challenged.

Just then yet another security guard walked in and flashed the lights on and off, as though he were trying to get the attention of the dead.

"Bed check in ten minutes. That's all for tonight fellas."

As the crowd broke up I wandered over to Billy. "What's a bed check?"

"They look to see if you're in your rack. It's done in all the better prisons."

"Wait, Billy, I thought this was a shelter."

"Matter of perspective," he said and headed off towards the dormitory. I followed like the fool I wasn't, or didn't think I was.

Bunk 19A all mine, my little domicile for eight hours on my first day without a place to live. I was exhausted and still scared to death. How much longer would this last? How would I go about getting a job with no home address or decent clothes. What would happen when my seven days were up? I knew I couldn't live on the street, but I had to get tougher. Maybe Billy could be my street teacher, but I couldn't depend on him. Nothing is dependable, when you are homeless.

"Hey look who's my bunk mate," exclaimed Big Ray in that ever cheerful basso profundo of his. (Big man, big voice).

"Hey Ray, what did you think of my little pool match?"

"Mormons aren't allowed to gamble, but I was glad you waxed his tail."

"Thanks Pal, get a good night's sleep."

"Always do, say your name again is?"

"Don, just Don." I yawned

"Well," Ray concluded, "sleep well my friend."

I didn't sleep well. Fear and insomnia are twins that travel the midnight streets together. It didn't help that Ray snored louder than a 19th century freight train badly in need of an oil job. Finally, at about 3:00 in the morning, three of the security guards man hauled him outside and I think I nodded off after that. One day down, how much time I had left was as unknown as the empty blackness which I finally found.

CHAPTER NINE
Panic in the Year Zero

Nerves. Five days had passed, I was two days away from the street and mine were badly frayed. It had been five days of essentially doing nothing. Every morning I would give up frightful percentage of my net worth for a copy of the Albuquerque Journal and rip through the employment ads. There were openings, unfortunately most of them were for positions for which I wasn't remotely qualified. The closest I had come was a peculiar advertisement for a perfume salesman.

At first, it seemed like something I could do. Be charming, meet women, but the recruiter was less than enthused with my attire which was not a striped double breasted suit replete with tie and handkerchief. In addition, I think she was looking for a boyfriend who could sell perfume, and the thirty year difference in our ages did not work to my advantage.

So here I was two days away from being thrust on the streets with no a single place to sleep and the fear was welling up inside. I was a human volcano filled with pyroclastic terror. Billy could see it, Big Ray spent an inordinate amount of time trying to keep me calm.

"You got to get your shit together," Billy said. "Ain't no way you can make it on the streets. As you are now, I don't think you'd last 24 hours."

"I know." I replied very quietly.

51

"No you don't know. Every week, and I mean every fucking week somebody dies. Most of the time, they don't have ID and no one knows who they are or where they come from. All they did in their lives, the people they were, the folks they wanted to be, is reduced to zero.

"You don't read about it in the paper, because no one cares. Body goes down to the morgue, gets buried in a poor man's grave which no one will ever visit, because they don't know who the fuck is buried there.

"That my friend is the end of the line for the homeless. It is oblivion and I don't think you're ready for that – not yet."

Listening to Billy I felt seriously close to death, but at that point I didn't know what it meant to be a breath away from eternity. That would come later.

During the past five days a mustachioed gentleman named Richard joined our little clique. In his other life, Richard had been a manufacturer's representative for a line of women's clothing. He was good looking, had a certain charm, but had lost one too many battles with the bottle and a couple of divorce lawyers, not necessarily in that order.

"Took me for every fucking cent," was his constant, if somewhat almost unintelligible refrain, and normally I would have found it pretty off-putting, but the familiarity of the song struck a responsive chord so I cut Richard a considerable amount of slack. On the other hand, Richard had his ear to the ground – perhaps listening for the distinctive sound of a liquor truck - and on the morning of the sixth day, he joined Billy and me at breakfast.

"This could save our asses," he whispered. "Can't talk about it here; if this gets out it'll be like the Oklahoma Land Rush. Meet me in front of the library on 5th Street at 8:15 sharp."

"The library doesn't open until ten." Big Ray reminded him.

"This isn't about reading a book, Ray. It's about a place where we can spend the next month in relative luxury at the Hyatt Regency of homeless shelters."

Well that's all I needed to hear, the Hyatt Regency of Homeless Shelters, and even though I couldn't understand the reasoning behind it, Big Ray, Billy and I took a different route to the library so it wouldn't seem as though we were accompanying Richard. Something smelled fishy to me and there wasn't a fish market in sight, but I was desperate and so were my companions. None of us wanted to become street fodder for the University Avenue Desperados, we circled around a large downtown park three times to waste an hour, meeting Richard at precisely 8:15.

Forming a tight circle, Richard briefed us as though we were going into the Battle of the Bulge.

"Okay, of all the shelters that take men, the most desirable is a place called the Albuquerque Opportunity Center, which we'll call AOC," he whispered while looking from side to side making sure our secret intelligence wasn't compromised.

Fine, now the shelters were getting code names and we were in the CIA.

"The deal is, everybody wants to get in there. Nice beds, they'll help you find work and even a permanent home. They've got big screen TV and a storage room so you don't have to drag your personal items all over town."

He had a point there. Nothing makes you look more conspicuously homeless than one humungous travel bag. You look like a poverty stricken traveler on a vacation that will never end.

"To continue," Richard continued, "you can stay for 30 days, but if you find a job they'll give you up to 60 days; in some cases they even pay a cleaning deposit. Now the only way to get in is to make a reservation by phone at exactly 8:30. The phone number is 553-2323. Does everybody have a cell phone?"

Come on, this was 2007, that was like asking if everybody had a liver.

"So," Richard went on, "the way I hear it is that they're discharging about eleven guys today. That gives us a shot, but we all have start calling at 8:29."

Richard looked at his watch.

"In two minutes. I figure they have multiple lines and if we keep dialing we should get in."

Could we all make it through? Surely we weren't the only bums, uh homeless men, that knew about AOC, but anything was better than getting knifed by some miscreant while trying to sleep in the gutter somewhere. Besides I liked the name of the shelter, Albuquerque Opportunity Center. Opportunity was something I badly needed, and so did my friends.

At 8:29:25 we all started dialing. First try and I get a recorded message. Second try – a busy signal. I looked over at Richard, twenty feet away and he was talking on the phone nodding his head up and down, and motioning for the rest of us to come over.

"Her name is Deanna and she'll take your names. We're in baby, what did I tell you? In like fuckin' Flynn"

Richard handed me the phone and I politely gave my name to Deanna who had a thick Hispanic accent. Didn't bother me, as far as I was concerned she was Queen Isabella. Billy and Big Ray followed.

"Okay," Richard instructed, "we can't walk there, something about the neighbors freaking out if they actually see homeless guys. What do they expect at a homeless shelter? Maybe it's fronting as a make-under."
Everybody laughed Richard could be very funny.

"At 6:00 a bus will pick us up at the Mission right after dinner. They'll have our names and will take us to the Opportunity Center, and without prompting – believe me without prompting - we began singing a gospel song called: "Land of Opportunity Oh Lord Oh Lord."

Once we quieted down, I jumped in with a tad less enthusiasm.

"That's just great, even without the singing!"

I was so happy, it was like the knot that had taken up permanent residence in my stomach had been untied, but wait, suppose they made a mistake and didn't take down my name correctly. Well, I could theoretically run across the street to The Good Shepherd, if they hadn't already closed the gate. Something more to worry about, no worry isn't strong enough a word, obsess about. I was going to obsess about whether a woman named Deanna had placed my name on a list that some other stranger was going to read and admit me to the land of opportunity. Oh the opportunity for fuck ups.

Richard didn't seem worried at all.

"Hey, I got a couple of bucks, I'll get us a bottle." He offered.

"No wait, if we start drinking they might not let us in the place. Remember the Good Shepherd and its breathalyzer?"

"Don, you're going to grow old worrying."

Never mind the worrying, growing old was definitely part of my master plan. The other guys passed on the booze, but ever confident Richard with his Willy Lohman smile and a shoeshine bright as the morning star made a beeline for Central Avenue Liquors.

I waited for the library to open and contented myself in the periodical reading room until lunch, while Billy and Big Ray found a couple of computers and cruised the world wide web. Things were looking up. We'd found a place to stay, but then what?

CHAPTER TEN
Opportunity Knocks

Oh the Reverend Salvation was on a tare tonight. He was running fifteen minutes late. Seems like someone was giving him some attitude, so he made a speech about ungrateful wretches and threw the guy out of the mission.

"What about forgiveness?" A voice from the hungry multitudes piped up.

Apparently, forgiveness was reserved for God and Jesus because he didn't have any. Instead he berated all the sinners on Earth, and explained in detail how they would be tormented in hell for eternity, no - for longer than that.

The crowd was beginning to grumble as our ham hocks and turnip greens were moldering in the kitchen. Finally, he got off his lofty steed and proclaimed that we were all giving ourselves to the Lord that night and no one had the fearlessness to argue. It's hard to disagree on an empty stomach. As for me, I was worried we might be late for the bus which was to transport us to the Center of Opportunity.

I consumed my food like a hungry member of the lupine family. Big Ray was shoveling in the turnip greens as though he was stoking the boiler of a tramp steamer. After consuming enough southern food to insure a good case of gastric distress, Richard, Big Ray, Billy and I swarmed down the stairs to be first in line for the big yellow bus we were promised would arrive at 6:00.

At 6:01 I was convinced the bus had been hijacked by terrorists and was being taken to Juarez, where it would be dismantled and sold for parts. But no, with a cough, a sputter and a hiccup it appeared at the corner and slowly came in for landing in front of the mission. The spring loaded door snapped open and a freckled guy with a clipboard alighted.

I had crossed my fingers on both hands and would have crossed my legs too, but I would not have remained upright with my heavy suitcase. Please, my name had to be on his list. I waited. He called Billy, who smiled at him as he got onto the bus, then Richard and Big Ray, who took up an entire seat. I was sweating bullets, big one's .44 magnums, when he called my name next to last.

"Thank goodness," I said as I got onto the bus and into the seat up front, which it appeared I was going to share with the hero of the hour.

He smiled broadly, "Not to worry, we don't make mistakes, do we Julio?" He asked the bus driver.

"Only every day," replied the driver reaching new levels of laconic, which made me feel better and worse at the same time. What if my name dropped off the list, fell on the floor and was stuffed in some unreachable cubby?

At the freckled guy's direction, Julio closed the door and the ancient bus, which was probably listed on the national directory of old school busses, farted once and began to move. Suddenly, I felt my stomach relax. I doubted seriously they'd throw me from a moving vehicle.

"My name is Patrick," The bus boss said extending his hand.
"Call me Don," I said, returning the handshake.

"How long have you been homeless?" He asked.

"I've spent the last five days at the Good Shepherd, before then I stayed at a Motel 1 for a couple of months. I tried finding work, but…"

He nodded, "Work is tough to find these days, lots of unemployment. Well, we have a bed for you for the next month, perhaps you'll get a job and be well on your way to a normal life again."

I grinned. "As my Grandmother used to say, 'From your mouth to God's ear.'"

"That's funny, my Grandmother used to say the same thing." Patrick replied.

"Well, I'm glad we have something in common, Patrick, even if it is only grandmothers."

Patrick suppressed a grin – not very well.

"When we arrive you'll need to go to an orientation meeting for first timers, then you can watch television or read a book. Whatever you want. We're a safe, friendly, shelter."

A safe friendly shelter, I wondered if that meant no more breathalyzer tests and security guards following you around like you had Al Qaeda tattooed on both sides of your ass. In the back of the bus someone was playing a harmonica, a wistful melody that reminded me of the hollows of Eastern Kentucky. The conversation was lively, and seemed to be about someone named "Old Tex." We passed a homeless couple with a young child and immediately I felt guilty. They had no shelter, and were undoubtedly looking for a place to spend the night. Angry gray clouds were gathering over the mountains.

I pointed the family out to Patrick. "It breaks my heart," he said. "We have at least 3,000 homeless in Albuquerque and only enough beds for 10%. I'd take them all in if I could."

My God, this man had a soul, I thought. I wonder what brought him to this coliseum of sadness. The bus continued north, passing under Interstate 40, a well-known, highly dangerous area for homeless street people to sleep. A decrepit school building passed to our right and after a few turns we entered a long driveway that ended with a chain link fence.

Patrick jumped off the bus and rolled the rusting fence back to reveal an opening and the bus pulled through and parked next to three other busses, all of which had designs on the old bus home, where they could rust out their lives in peace, perhaps thinking, if busses can think, about all the schoolchildren that had decorated their seats with equal amounts of promise and mischief. As we pulled to a stop, he jumped back on the bus and announced:

"All first time residents report to the office. For the rest of you: Welcome to the Albuquerque Opportunity Center."

So, this was AOC, a huge building that looked like it had been a warehouse at one time. I guess I was to be part of its current inventory. I had the sense that an adventure lay ahead. I was hoping for one that culminated in a return to the life I had known, but nothing could be further from the truth. The time horizon of the future is the ultimate unknowable.

CHAPTER ELEVEN
AOC

The small office belied the size of the place. There were two desks and each of us newbies, in turn, sat before the man at the desk and gave up the information of our lives, from where we were born to what kind of religious ceremony would be like performed in the unlikely-hood of our deaths. It was all done very professionally, there were no attempts at humor.

It was explained to us that this information would be part of a database. AOC wasn't simply in the business of temporarily warehousing people with no place to stay. It was the non profit organization's mission to "end homelessness – forever," at least in Albuquerque. I didn't see at the time how such a noble sentiment could be carried out, not in this time or society, but then it occurred to me that organizations such as this didn't exist in the plip of time allotted to humans. They could span centuries picking away at the problem, as though they had miner's axes, until one day in the distant future they would strike gold. What a day that would be! No shelters, no homeless, no people living on the edge of nothingness, and most of all, human lives driven with a purpose, however personal or arcane it might be.

After giving us a supply of towels, washcloths, razors, shampoo, skin cream(!), toothbrushes and toothpaste, we were escorted into the dormitory. Before us were 74 beds all discretely separated by furnishings with built in drawers to hold underwear and other private matters. All four of us newbies were taken to an open lounge where I correctly assumed our orientation would be held.

A group of chairs were arranged in a semi-circle with the head chair reserved for Patrick, who sat down and smiled at every one of us.

"There's a packet of information for each of you. Please don't read it now, it will put you to sleep."

A twitter of appreciative laughter followed.

"Welcome to Albuquerque Opportunity Center. You'll notice the word shelter doesn't appear in our name, though it is part of our guiding purpose. Each night we shelter 74 men from the terrible conditions of the streets. For the next thirty days you'll each have your own beds. Nobody can take those away from you except you yourself. If somebody tries or claims your bed is his, we'll straighten things out quietly.

"This is not a place for fights. If it's fighting your looking for, or just bullying for that matter, there's plenty of that outside, and believe me you don't want any part of it. AOC is a place for your to get your heads back together, find work and a safe place to live. Now, we don't expect you to do all that on your own, we're here to help.

"We have counselors, outplacement specialists and employment experts who will make appointments with you, appointments you are expected to keep, and provide whatever services we can. Generally speaking, from 30-40% of all our residents obtain come kind of employment and a clean, safe place to call home."

"How do we know if you can help us?" Big Ray spoke up.

"Simple, by going along with the program and doing the best you can, whether by following our rules or cooperating with the counselors. Men, we're on your side. Everyone of you that walks out of here and back into a better life is a victory for us. You don't know how wonderful it feels for every success story we amass.

"Now, to be honest, there are those who are doomed to spend their lives on the streets. For the most part these are people addicted to drugs or are so mentally unstable that they wish to remove themselves from society in general. At the present time we don't have a solution, or an easy transition for these men. They were lost to us long before they ever got their thirty days.

"Unlike some other residence facilities, we don't burden you with list upon list of rules and regulations, but we have a few."

That brought a smile from everybody.

"First on our list is no drugs, other than prescription medication and you'd better show us the bottle with the doctor's name just like you get from the drug store. Second, no weapons of any kind. We have people here to help you if you get in a hassle with someone. If somebody pushes you and you draw a knife, you will be banned from the premises. That's right, we'll put you out on the street, because if you're weaponed, that's where you belong. If you both pull a knife, the police are called you'll be banned and will both go to jail. No ifs, ands, or buts. This is a peaceful place, we look to our residents to keep it that way.

"For your recreation there are books in our library and dozens of movies to watch on the big screen TV. If a movie is on you will not interfere with it, no rallying the troops to get it shut off. Deal with it until it's your turn to select a different title.

"Lastly, when lights go down at 9:30 we expect quiet. Men have had a long day on the street and mostly they need rest. If you feel the need to smoke a Native, go outside on the patio and make sure to close the door. Our backyard was xeroscaped for your viewing pleasure. Make sure your butts go in the can, or you'll find yourself cleaning the entire yard by yourself.

"We try to run a modern facility built on good manners. Our job is to get you back to the life you knew. If there are questions or anything that myself or the Resident Advisors (we have no security goons around here) can do to help you, please talk to us. If you have a complaint it will be dealt with. Most especially, if you want to say something nice, we're ready to listen, because for the staff, that's what makes this work worthwhile, that and the restoration of your lives. So take your paperwork, find your bunk and may you pass a restful evening."

The men gave Patrick a standing ovation. Finally, a place that treats us like human beings and not the dregs of society. I decided to get a meeting with a job counselor the next day. More than anything I wanted my life back, I wanted to be somebody again, I wanted the fulfillment I had known in what now seemed like the distant past.

Like an uninvited ghost the words "You can never go home again" cannonaded across my mind. It occurred to me, after all, just because a famous writer says something doesn't make it so. I never stopped to think that those words were less the mental gymnastics of a well known author, and more the world-life experiences of generations the writer had never known.

CHAPTER TWELVE
If It's Too Good to Be True

Four days later I met with the employment counselor, it seems he had a bit of a backlog. Hmmm, he poured through his computer printouts and newspaper ads.

"Ever worked retail?" He asked.

"Sure, when I worked for Do Re Mi Music while I was going to high school."

"You're a little long in the tooth for retail." He concluded. I checked the length of my front teeth with my tongue.

"Wait a minute," his excited voice brought my invisible dental check to an end. "You worked in television."

"That's right. Most of my life."

"Do you know what a promo editor is?"

Now I was excited. "I spent about a third of my life in edit bays; I've probably edited a couple hundred promos."

"Terrific, then you're perfect. There's a local station looking for a promo editor. How about if I set up an interview for you?"

64

"Do it. I'm your man, uh their man." I said with total enthusiasm.

He promised to get back to me once he'd made some calls. Imagine, a promo editor; now I'd long since moved beyond that level of work, but hey work was what I was after. As Billy had said, "I would have to work my way off the streets."

The very next day I was sitting in the cleanest clothes I had left, a Don Ho Hawaiian Shirt, in the lobby of the television station, miles, no make it light years from the shelter. Everything seemed so familiar, perhaps I'd come home. The receptionist gave me a five page form to fill out that included everything I'd ever done remotely related to TV, like pulling the plug as well as turning it on and off. I probably gave her one of the most comprehensive employment applications she'd ever seen.

A half hour passed and a balding gentleman in a slick suit the color of a UPS truck came out and motioned for me to follow him. I wasn't terribly nervous about doing an interview; after all, in my other life I had pitched shows to the presidents of television networks and movie studios. I had to turn my head around as fast as humanly possible. I could no longer think of myself as a homeless waif, but had to project the image of an experienced producer / director, one who could get the job done with as little hassle as possible.

We arrived in the office of the Promotions Manager while Mr. UPS took his seat. He scanned my application then removed his glasses and wiped the lenses.

"I've been in local television for nearly 25 years and I've never seen an application like this." He mused. "You worked for Dick Clark?"

"Yes, I spent four years in Dick's shop. Went from a researcher to director – also ran his archives." Was I being humble enough?

"So you did network programming?" he pushed.

65

"Everywhere but Fox, it hadn't started up back in the 80's." I responded cheerfully.

"…and Carson Company, would that be Johnny Carson?" He asked rather tentatively.

"Yes, since he died it's run by his brother Dick." I felt myself sinking into a quagmire of TMI (too much information).

"Well, Mr. Barrett," he began (a bad sign – he was talking to me as though I was his boss), "if you don't mind my asking, what are you doing here?"

"It's a long story. I burned out on Hollywood, not the first, and I'm not the last."

"Burned out on Hollywood? It appears you burned out on Las Vegas as well." I knew where this was going and I didn't like it.

"Bad divorce, I was married to a lawyer." Now that should have explained everything but it didn't.

"Well, sir, it appears you have more television experience than all the people at this station put together. The guy you'd be working for is 23 years old, just out of the University of New Mexico."

"Look, the truth is I need the work…" It shouldn't be hard to defend the truth, but often it's impossible.

"…and I need somebody who isn't marking time waiting for a call from our headquarters in New York as the new Vice President of Programming. Mr. Barrett, you are seriously over-qualified for this work."

"That may be, but think of what a good job I can do for you."

"Hmmm, perhaps, but we still have some people to interview."

I figured that was the end. I might as well be gracious maybe someday they'd need someone who knew what they were doing.

"I understand your predicament, it's a shame my over-qualification can't be used to help you."

"We'll keep your name on file," Mr. Promotions didn't promise. With that cliché ringing in my ears, he escorted me to the lobby and held open the door.

I suppose if things are too good to be true, they are, the question was: where am I going to find a situation in Albuquerque for which I'm not overqualified. I wonder if the Promotions Manager could see the way I hung my head on the long eleven block walk back to the bus stop. It was the longest walk of my entire life.

CHAPTER THIRTEEN
Now You've Really Got Trouble

There's a saying on the street that goes something like, "If you think you've got trouble now, just wait until you've really got trouble." It sounds a bit like circumlocution but what it really means is as bad as being homeless is, it doesn't compare to being homeless and losing your health.

As Billy once put it, "This is one time in your life you don't want to get sick or it could be the last time in your life you get sick."

Two weeks had flown, since my promotion editor job interview. There was a strange phone call from the station's Vice President of Operations saying they "were building a new facility and might get back to me." Well, if that was hope, it was being dispensed with a miserliness of Scroogian proportions. I remember laying in bed waiting for lights out and feeling rather sorry for myself. How would I ever get my life back was the question that just kept circling my mind like a single engine plane low on gas, waiting for permission to land – and there was no landing strip.

Then it hit me. It was a pain in my chest that brought tears to my eyes and immediately what I could see of the dormitory was tilting at a crazy angle. I tried to sit up but that was an act of futility, instead I fell back and hit my head on the wall next to me. Then I began to vomit.

"Oh shit," some nameless resident exclaimed, "This sucker is puking his guts out. Somebody do something."

68

Realizing it was me, Billy raced over, yelling, "Hey Big Ray, get your ass over here. We got a friend in need."

Ignoring the smell which must have been atrocious, Billy and Ray tried to get me to sit up.

"Get some water over here." He yelled to no one in particular, but almost immediately one of the Resident Advisors was over in a flash.

"I don't like his color," he said. Picking up his walkie-talkie, "Call 911 I think we got a problem here, bed 39 lower bunk."

"You're going to be okay," Billy reassured me. "They're going to get you some medical attention."

I could barely speak. "Please make sure my stuff is put in storage I have almost nothing…"

"Don't you worry none," Billy replied.

In the distance I could just make out the sound of a siren that was growing louder with every breath I tried to take. The room was going dim and then bright.

"Who's playing with the lights." I screamed, as the sound of the siren filled my brain.

Suddenly, the door nearest my bed burst open and three Emergency Medical Techs strode in, trailing equipment, parting the sea of on-lookers shouting directions. Now I was the center of everybody's attention and I didn't like it one bit.

"Give these men some room, Goddamn it." Billy shouted, as one of the EMT's wrapped a blood pressure cuff around my left arm, while another pressed a stethoscope up to my chest.

"What are you feeling?" The EMT asked quietly. I could barely hear him. "What's his name."

"His name is Don." Billy said – anger in his voice.

"Don, what are you feeling?" The EMT yelled at me.

"Pressure, pain." Was all I could get out.

"BP is 165/130, pulse is thready – let's get him out of here." The lead EMT ordered, as a gurney was wheeled beside the bed.

It was like looking through a fish eye lens, everyone was staring at me, I'm sure most of them hoping I was okay, but I knew all of them were thankful it wasn't they who were the object of all this medical attention. No - anything but that.

The safety belts on the gurney were snapped shut and I could feel it move. It was like being on a ride at an amusement park, faster and faster they wheeled me. The overhead lights whizzed by like passing trains. I flashed on the opening of an old TV show, "Ben Casey." Then I felt the sting of the cold air outside as they lifted the gurney and loaded me in the back of a shit wagon. That's what they called them on the street: shit wagons, because if you were in one, you were in a world of shit.

"Don, do you have insurance?" One of the techs shouted at me.

"No."

"UNMH" (University of New Mexico Hospital) he shouted to the driver.

"Just stay calm Don." He tried to soothe me but I wasn't in any shape to appreciate it. "Where's your ID."

"Wallet right rear pocket."

He collected my wallet and began going through it, writing down information off my driver's license and whatever else he found.

I remember hearing the siren and feeling the movement of the vehicle. I kept trying to say something to the EMT but nothing intelligible was coming out.

"Don't try to talk, Don. Just stay c…a…l."

Silence.

"Don, Don, open your eyes. Do you know where you are?" A voice screamed.

"Van?" I guessed startled out of my mind.

A man was standing over me. He was wearing a set of blue scrubs. There were intravenous lines going into my right arm and I could feel the squeeze of a blood pressure cuff inflating on my left arm. The light was blinding and I tried to close my eyes and shut it out, but the man in the scrubs continued to yell my name.

"When did they put those things in me?"

"Don, you're in the ER at University Hospital. You've had a heart attack. We're doing some tests while we find you a room. You're going to be our guest for a little while. How are you feeling?"

"Out of it." I wasn't sure what "it" was but my consciousness was all over the place. I felt a little like the moment before you fall asleep, still conscious, aware of your surroundings and then bam it's the next morning, but I wasn't dozing off.

In the distance I could hear somebody screaming in pain, and then the screaming stopped abruptly.

"Did somebody just die?" I asked with the innocence of a five year old.

"No, we just gave him something for his pain. We try not to lose people in this ER," the man in the scrubs said matter-of-factly.

"Don't lose me." I answered. Was I making a joke? Even now, was I trying to deflect my fear with humor? Not surprising – it was something I had done all my life. Laugh and the fear goes away, but I was more afraid than I can ever remember, and there was nothing to laugh about.

At that moment, two nurses and a doctor came into the room. When you're a patient, you assume everybody is either a doctor or nurse. Of course, that isn't true, but it's a comforting thought.

One came over and put his hand on my upper arm. It was strangely comforting to be touched by somebody not wearing latex. There was no barrier between us.

"I'm Dr. Alameda, welcome to my ER." He said with all the authority in the world.

"How do you do doctor, you know I don't remember coming into the hospital." The words were dry in my throat, I could barely get them out.

"Mr. Barrett, just as you were arriving you coded. That's doctor speak meaning your heart stopped. The EMT's shocked it back into operation, now we've got to do a bunch of tests to make sure it keeps going."

"You mean I was dead?" I asked incredulously.

"Let's just say you looked the old man square in the eye and he blinked. You're a pretty tough hombre."

He was being kind, of course, I was no tougher than anybody else whose heart had stopped. I lay there trying to process the thought that for a moment I was dead. I'd never spent any real time thinking about death, dissecting non-existence; I'd certainly never obsessed about it the way Woody Allen did in his films. Now it was a shadow, a doppelganger forever haunting me, I could never go back. What would happen the next time I coded? What if there were no EMT's with their electric paddles? I started to cry. I might never see my daughter again. Oh my poor Torrey, I didn't want it to be this way. I wanted you to understand that I have always loved you. You weren't the reason your mom and I broke up.

The doctor wiped away the tear flowing down my cheek. "You're going to be alright. That's our job around here to make sure you are. You've got your life back, Mr. Barrett, now you need to work with us to hang onto it."

CHAPTER FOURTEEN
The Sticks and the Blurs

The next few days were a blur of tests, tests, and more tests. Shots abounded. I don't know about you, but I never liked getting shots. I remember as a boy being lined up in an elementary school class while they gave out Polio Shots (this was the original Salk vaccine). Of course it was a blessing, but I still remember what seemed like a lot of pain (to a nine year old it is – all things in considered). The truth is, I still don't like shots, but you get to a certain age or a particular condition and they become part of your way of life.

I was in a private room on the seventh floor of UNMH (University of New Mexico Hospital). The only visitors I had were doctors, nurses, orderlies, techs, and whoever wandered by. I felt so totally alone. I tried calling Jackie to tell her about my present situation only to have her remind me we were divorced. Apparently twenty years of marriage wasn't worth even a millisecond's worth of sympathy. The big question kept rolling through my head: What would become of me?

About the only highlights to my day were when someone would come in, put me in a wheel chair and roll me to another department for testing. The stress test was particularly interesting. In my condition they couldn't exactly put me on a treadmill, so instead they gave me an injection that made me feel just awful. I was filled with anxiety and stress, but I had two technicians around who told me to stick with it. After about ten minutes of this subtle form of torture, they gave me another injection and within moments I felt just fine. Wow, was this chemical heart attack developed by the CIA to use on prisoners? Seriously, one minute you think you are dying and the next everything is fine.

Then, back into the wheelchair and upstairs to my room. My only entertainment was the television. I had 96 cable channels and each seemed to be filled with one obnoxious commercial after another. I was so bored though that I was willing to watch anything even an infomercial for a broom. For 28 minutes this guy was so excited by what this broom could do, I thought he was going to have an orgasm right on camera. He kept saying over and over that if he never owned another broom, this would be his to the day he died. Imagine in the real world, devoting that kind of loyalty to a broom. I would have been ashamed to make a commercial that insipid, but then which of us was earning a living, me or the broom guy? (By this point, I was down to $1.12 and in debt).

The most difficult and certainly the most invasive test was something called an angiogram. This is where they inject a contrast agent usually through the femoral artery, which flows through the body and up into the coronary arteries. Then using an x-ray based technique they determine just how blocked those arteries may be. I don't know about anybody else, but I was at least semi-awake through the whole procedure, although I can't confess to feeling any pain (discomfort yes).

Then when the angiogram was completed I was wheeled back into the alabaster chamber that served as my room. At this time I was clueless in terms of what might be wrong with me, in fact, I did my best to block everything out of my mind. My brain sent me to a different happier place with a little help from my friends.

I was on the half-day boat out of Long Beach, California fishing for whatever came my way. After puking my guts out on Super Coola, an unpopular but cheap drink of the time, I remember catching the biggest fish of my life to date. It was a three pound mackerel, which I was determined to cook when we got home. We fried it up in a pan and discovered it was mostly bone and not enough meat to keep a poodle alive for an hour. All my Uncles and mother as well, had a good laugh over that. It was my first big disappointment as a would-be fisherman.

"Don," the voice said and shook me awake. There were two people standing in the room. One was apparently the doctor still wearing greens, the other was dressed in civilian clothes and stood a good three feet behind the doctor, barely detectable within my field of view.

"Don," the doc began, "Our angiogram yielded these pictures."

He handed a stack of pictures to me. They looked like highways shot from orbit, but it quickly dawned on me that in fact they were blood vessels.

He pointed four of the arteries out to me.

"These are coronary arteries; they supply blood to your heart. I am sorry to tell you that they are completely blocked.

"So what's the bad news?" I asked.

Annoyed at being interrupted:

"The good news is: this is 2007 and we can replace those blood vessels with nearly identical ones from your arms and legs."

"Fine, go ahead." Was the only thing I could think of saying.

"There is a problem, Don, and I'm going to let Ms. Canfield explain it."

Ms. Canfield came forward. She looked in her forties with a sad expression etched on her face from years of delivering bad news.

"The trouble is, Mr. Barrett, this kind of operation takes up to a year from which to recover. There are no facilities in New Mexico available to you and without a place to recover, the operation can't be performed."

"What does that mean?" I asked, not really wanting to hear the answer.

The doctor stepped back up to a position of alpha primacy. "I'm afraid it means we can't keep you in the hospital. We're arranging your discharge tomorrow."

"No, doctor, what does it mean to me?"

"Without the surgery, your heart will become starved of oxygen and cease to function."

"How much time do I have, please be honest with me." I begged.

The doctor frowned and thought for what seemed like an eternity.

"Perhaps a month."

Canfield broke in, "I'm sorry, it's just the system."

"So the system is going to let me die like a dog and do nothing. With all due respects fuck your system."

CHAPTER FIFTEEN
So I was a Dead Man Walking

"...so that's the way it is, Billy. I've got maybe a month and then I'm just going to keel over."

"That's the most fucked up thing I've ever heard." Billy was walking beside me on the way to breakfast at the Mission.

"I'm going to the library after we eat, to see if there's somewhere that will take me. I don't want to drop dead on the street and be buried in a potter's field."

Tears were welling up in Billy's brown eyes, he turned his head away so it wouldn't show, but you can't turn your head that far.

"What if you're feeling woozy and we just call 911?"

"They won't keep me in the ER unless I'm unconscious."

"This is the damndest thing I ever heard of. Why you? What have you done to deserve this?" He thundered.

"Come on Billy, bad things happen to good people all the time. At least the shelter has promised to keep a bed open for me, as long as I..." I was just too choked up to go on. Besides we were in the dining hall and I didn't want to share my feelings with the entire group.

"Hey 8-Ball," someone shouted, remembering my feat at the pool table. I just waved a hand at the sound, then began spooning scrambled eggs in my plate. My mind was a blank. Maybe I could find a place for dying homeless strangers on the internet, but somehow I doubted it. I lost track of time. Billy had drifted away, probably having a smoke, and I left the dining hall and the mission, violating street rule 101, don't go anywhere by yourself. At that moment, I didn't care.

I was walking down 4th street not particularly aware of my surrounding. About a block ahead of me a black teenage kid was walking and shadow boxing. The quickness of his movements, the way he darted and danced should have clued me that he was on something, probably speed. When I was his age, about the worse thing you could do was sneak a beer, but I was never much about drinking. Then in college pot came in and yes, I liked it, but I never went beyond. I had friends doing coke, acid, bennies, poppers, but honestly I was afraid of hard drugs. Of course, there was always heroine, but in those days you couldn't have paid me to stick a needle in my arm. Now the docs were doing it as though it were an Olympic sport.

I was totally out of touch with the modern drug culture. I had enough trouble sleeping, amphetamines were the last thing I would ever have tried. That's why I wasn't thinking that a kid on speed might be dangerous to me.

Next thing I know he's walking over to me, still shadow boxing. I did my best to keep walking, but he wanted to have some fun with an old man.

"Hey man, what's that cap. You from Los Angeles?"

"Yeah, born and bred in LA." I answered.

"You know out here that's a gang affiliation. You ain't no gangsta mista?"

"I'm too old, they wouldn't take me."

"I could take you, like that!" The little bastard taunted by snapping his fingers. He threw a left hook at the bill of my cap. It fell to the ground. I reached down and picked it up. He knocked it off again. I thought about kicking him right in the balls, but before I could gain position, the kid hit me square on the right side of my jaw. For some reason I didn't flinch.

"You pretty tough for an old guy. Maybe I shouldn't be fucking with you. You might have been on one of those killer one death squads in Vietnam." He said as I was preparing to get the crap knocked out of me.

"You go on your way. Billy Bo Lightning don't need to beat up old men."

I got to the library and sat on the step. My jaw was beginning to swell. Big Ray ambled by.

"Hey Don, how you feeling...what happened?"

"Some punk tried to use me for a punching bag."

"This punk got a name?" Ray asked pointedly.

"Something like Billy Bo Lightning. He's probably long gone now, nothing much to do about it. Just another piece of crap on the street."

"Can you describe him – humor me."

"Yeah Ray, about five foot nine, black, wearing shorts, walking around like he was shadow boxing. Probably on speed. I'd stay away from him if I were you."

"There isn't a five foot nine kid that can put the hurt on a 6 foot 6 350 lb. hunk of man. See you around Don."

Ray went off looking for the kid. I doubted he'd find him. My jaw began to throb, I could feel some blood trickling down my lip. Not much to worry about when you've got a month to live – maybe a month, maybe a week, who knows.

At 10:00 the library opened and I began a three hour pathetic search for – what can I call it? An old elephant burial ground? I found a few places in Louisiana and Mississippi – basically publically funded old folks homes, but they had no medical capability and were just warehouses for elderly people with no place to go. According to the age requirements I was too young, and with $1.12 left in my pocket I had no way of reaching them. They may just as well have been located on a moon of Jupiter. It was very depressing and my stomach began to grumble, but in my desperation to find a place to die, I had neglected noon day lunch at the first Baptist Church. Now there would be nothing until 5:00 at the Mission.

I decided to take a walk over to 7-11. Occasionally a homeless person with enough to buy a sandwich would sit on a low wall that ran beside the store. Maybe I could get a piece of cheese.

There was nobody on the street, but I did see Billy and Big Ray coming from the direction of fifth street. Big Ray had a smile the size of Utah, and the punk in hand, so I knew something had happened.

"Found 'em." Billy said immediately.

"The punk who…" I started.

"The very same one." Big Ray finished. "Seems he was having some 'fun' with an old guy confined to a wheel chair. Billy came up behind him and I swung around from the side. I said, 'Hey Mr. Boxer take a punch at me.' Of course he backed away, and Billy grabbed him under the chin and pulled him off balance."

Now they had the kid right before my eyes. Billy pointed at me. "This man look familiar to you?"

"Nah, all whitties look the same to me."

Billy took one arm and Big Ray the other and they walked the boy behind an alley; I decided not to go with them.

The story goes: there was no one else around, mostly because an open dumpster, surrounded with flies was stinking to high heaven.

Billy pinned the punk against the dumpster.

"That man you hit, you know the whitey you didn't know, he's dying from heart failure."

"Not my problem." The kid blustered.

"Well this is," said Big Ray as he drove his big meaty fist into the kid's middle. The boy doubled over only to have his nose meet Billy's knee. All three men could hear the crack as knee met nose and nose broke.

"Hey," the kid blurted, tears welling in his eyes, "I'm sorry, I didn't know he was a friend of yours."

"You should be in school, not picking fights with people who can't fight back." Billy said. "Hey Ray, why don't you show him that bear hug you was telling me about."

Ray folded his arms around the youth and slowly began to squeeze. You could hear the ribs popping on the next block, but on the streets people pretty much mind their own business.

"You had enough?" Ray whispered into the kids ear.

Barely breathing, and in desperate pain, the punk managed a yes.

Big Ray picked up the boy and threw him into the dumpster and pulled down the lid. "Maybe someone will hear him screaming and maybe they won't."

"Ray, you are one mean motherfucker."

"I did worse things in the Army." Was all Ray would reply. "Let's find Don and tell him the good news."

"I expect any news is good news when you're in his shape." Billy nodded, and the two of them went off looking for me.

After hearing the story all I could think to say was, "I hope you didn't kill him."

"Well, that's life." Said Billy without a trace of irony.

CHAPTER SIXTEEN
There's a Chance

Dinner at the Mission was unexceptional. Chicken croquets and corn were the cuisine d'jour. Nobody said much, I was in a funk, and I think Billy and Ray were having second thoughts about the street justice they'd handed out. We'd heard nothing about police finding a beat up black kid in a dumpster; just as well, I had enough on my plate spending time thinking how the end would come. I hoped it would be in bed, that I'd just close my eyes and give myself to the Universe. Funny, how you can still care about embarrassing yourself in your last act on Earth.

There was a new face on the bus ride to the shelter, one who would become a major player in my story, although at that moment she was just a trainee learning the ropes. Shannon O'Keefe was taller than me, but had a sweetness to her face that made her uncommonly beautiful. Patrick introduced her to me.

"You're the one who had the heart attack." Was our rather awkward introduction.

"Yes. What a surprise."

She really didn't know how to react to my sarcasm, but began to ask me about my life. Maybe she was taking an interest in me, or perhaps I was the first homeless person with whom she'd had any real interaction. In many ways her life was more interesting than mine.

84

Shannon had done what very few people ever do. She received a Bachelor's Degree from the University of New Mexico without ever getting her high school diploma. Having accomplished such an unusual feat made her worth getting to know, at least for as long as I had left.

Then after checking his clipboard, Patrick piped up, "Don, Dennis wants to see you when we get in."

Dennis could only mean Dennis Plummer, the Executive Director of the Albuquerque Opportunity Center. He was like a wraith, rarely seen and nobody on the floor knew exactly what he did, except run the place, which had to be a complex job. What he wanted of me I couldn't fathom, and that was more than a little stressful. I'd been promised a bed to the very end, what could he want in return, my liver?

Well, I didn't have long to wait, because five minutes later we pulled through the chain link gate into the compound. I went ahead to the office, much to the curiosity of Billy and Big Ray. Perhaps this had something to do with the shadow boxer, but how would that involve Dennis?

Arriving at the office I told the Resident Assistant that Dennis wanted to see me.

He looked a little incredulous. "Dennis Plummer?"

"No Dennis the Menace." A dying man has the right to some sarcasm.

Not wanting to delve any deeper he walked me up a long flight of stairs to the second floor, a space forbidden to residents, the province of management and Resident Advisors. The RA knocked on the only closed door and Dennis emerged. He stuck out his hand and welcomed me.

"I'm Dennis Plummer the Executive Director, Don. I've been working to resolve your situation."

"I don't understand," and I didn't.

"Well, we've been considering an experiment for some months now. The idea is to take three beds out of play, wall them off to provide some privacy, and make them available 24 hours a day for those residents who are too sick to leave in the morning. In your situation, we'd like to offer you a place to recover from the surgery you need to have."

I couldn't believe what I was hearing. This man was handing me my life back.

"It won't be anything fancy. We still don't have the food situation worked out, but you'll have a bed, a chest of drawers, a lock box for your medications, and there will probably be visiting medical personnel."

"But this is wonderful, I was preparing to die…"

"I know and frankly your situation kicked this program into high gear. You may have to stay in the hospital longer than usual, since we don't have the facilities of a rest home, but we'll do the best we can to make you comfortable. We're going to build the space while you're in UNMH and it'll be ready when you come home. That's how I want you to think of this place – it's your home until you can get out on your own again. There is no time limit."

I was flabbergasted. "This is the best news I've had in three months. What can I say but thank you?"

"Your welcome, but this is a test for us. We'd like to be able to do more, so we have to see what happens with you and two other men we'll select. It's going to be called the Respite Care Program and if all works well, it'll save lives."

"You know, you're saving this one. I owe you."

Dennis shook his head. "Don't worry about owing anything. We've made an appointment with the cardiothoracic surgeon who will actually perform the operation. Then they have to schedule the OR and a room for you. This could be the start of a long process. Are you up for it?"

"The only other option I have is a short process and I'm not much interested in that. Let's do it, and thanks again to you and everyone involved."

"Okay, Don. Good luck." He shook my hand. What a mensch!

I was going to live! What greater gift could I ever hope to receive. I couldn't wait to tell the guys on the floor, but something in the back of my mind told me it wasn't going to be that simple. That damn little voice which sees reality for what it is and lives somewhere deep inside my brain, beyond the range of magnetic resonance, was right, as usual, simplicity was not in my future.

CHAPTER SEVENTEEN
The Handwriting on the Wall

The man on the other side of the desk didn't look particularly like a surgeon. He certainly wasn't dressed like one. Instead he wore a beautifully tailored suit with thin pin stripes, a blue oxford shirt and a conservatively striped tie. He had more the air of a CEO, than a man who manipulated organs and blood vessels.

He offered me a seat; within arms reach was a bottle of ice cold Fiji Water. In front of him was an opened file, rather thick, filled with a variety of forms and reports.

"You're a smart man, Mr. Barrett. You've worked most of your life in film and television and I see you have an advanced degree in musicology. You've left quite a trail on Google, which includes some acclaimed reviews of your work in the New York Times and Entertainment Weekly Magazine."

"I had no idea the hospital did this level of research on a homeless patient with a dying heart."

He smiled thinly. "Hospitals aren't the same as they were when your mother's brother was making 'Ben Casey' on ABC-TV. For example, as the head of your surgical team I'm more like a Chief Executive Officer in terms of what work will be performed on you. Dozens of people will receive instructions on your care directly or through their supervisors. Those instructions all begin with me. To misquote Harry Truman, I am where the buck stops.

"This will our last meeting of which you'll be conscious, of course I'll be by your side throughout the surgical procedure we call a cabbage."

"Cabbage?" I couldn't imagine what a quadruple bypass had to do with a leafy vegetable.

"No sir, it's an acronym. It stands for Coronary Artery Bypass Graft. In your case there will be four of them. We'll be taking arteries from other parts of your body and replacing the clogged arteries attached to your heart."

"It sounds enormously complicated."

"It is sir, a generation ago it couldn't be performed. Then we began using veins as our bypass media. Now we use arteries since they are tougher and tend to last longer."

"Which brings me doctor to the biggest question of them all. How much longer does this procedure give me, in terms of life span?" I wondered.

"Decades, Mr. Barrett, assuming you stick to a moderate diet, get some exercise, and take your medication without fail. There will be a dozen new prescriptions in your life, each of which is vital to prolonging it."

"So you're basically saying, 'don't mess up your good work.'"

"Not just my work. You're recovery depends on the cooperation of people down to the techs and those who service your hospital room. This is truly a team effort."

For the first time that day I could feel sweat running down my neck and pooling around my collar.

"First you need to know," the surgeon continued, "this will not be a pain free operation. To get to your heart we must break your breast bone and then fasten it back together. Then there is the medication we must give you to stabilize your heart, the most annoying of which is called Heparin and is shot directly into your stomach muscle every four hours. Following surgery, you'll be placed in ICU where we can monitor you closely and decide when you're ready to be moved to a normal hospital bed. The good news is that modern anesthesia uses drugs that tend to suppress any memory you may have of the procedure or the time you spend in ICU."

"And dare I ask what the bad news is?"

"This is a very serious operation and there are always chances of complications."

He went on to explain just about everything that could kill me and how I needed to put my affairs in order. Being homeless means your affairs are few and there's not much you can do to further disorder them. After another fifteen minutes of his time, which I am sure was valued by the hospital in the thousands of dollars per hour (and that was a ridiculous underestimation), it came down to the date.

He chose July 11, 2007 and if a date could sound lucky to somebody who wasn't particularly superstitious, 7-11-07 was as good as they come. That means I had ten days to get ready; ten days to prepare myself for a trauma beyond my wildest imagination. It was better that I didn't know what lay ahead, because I might have chosen a coward's way out.

CHAPTER EIGHTEEN
The Word on the Street

For the next ten days I was the most famous homeless person in all of Albuquerque. Everybody wanted to wish me luck. People in ragged clothing, pushing heavily laden shopping carts filled with their worldly possessions, were crossing the street to wish me God's speed. Others who were holding down day jobs, trying to work their way out of the strangle hold of poverty, were stopping by my bed at night, offering their hands in friendship.

"Hell, you're a goddamn celebrity!" Billy observed. "You're going to need someone like me just to handle the press."

"For some reason I don't think the reporters will be lined up."

"No, they're too busy covering drunk bus drivers, murderers and rapists. Besides, the public might not take too kindly to one of us getting a very expensive operation." He observed.

In all the excitement I'd forgotten what it would cost for an uninsured person to get what I was being given for nothing. My bill was paid by the state and reimbursed by the federal government.

"Don't I have a $5 co-pay." I asked and got a laugh.

"You don't have $5 chump. We'd have to take up a collection or I'd have to sell some of my blood. If they don't ask you don't offer. Could be somebody up there likes you."

"Likes me? Look what he's putting me through!" I was certain that God and I were not on good terms.

"Consider it an apology." Billy rejoined. "You're a hero on the street. Never been a homeless in Albuquerque who ever got a deal like this, not that I know of. You need a new heart? Better go dig yo'self a hole."

Everyday that passed, Shannon, the new RA, made a point of visiting with me. How was I doing? Could they do anything to make me more comfortable. Seems the RA's took up a collection and bought me Pajamas. Her Mom, who was a voracious reader would be bringing in books for me. Someone even scrounged up an extra pillow, since I'd be in bed most of the time. The entire homeless community seemed to be coming together over this one person who's heart was about to be cut open and repaired.

Funny thing though, a sophisticated viewer of the scene might think that some politician would use this to position themselves as the friend of the poor and disenfranchised. Not one word was heard from the Democrats, Republicans or any other party. It must be as Billy said, they were afraid of angering their constituents that tax money was being spent on someone deemed worthless.

That was the real irony. If I recovered from this surgery, really made it back all the way, I could work again. I might not be a hot shot television producer, but I'm sure I could do something to enrich the tax base. No, I was being tarred with the same stereotypical brush as the beggar on the street corner. Couldn't they understand that life, real life, wasn't "Leave it to Beaver." That good people could and did suffer personal disasters from which they couldn't recover without some kind of assistance. The people that ran the Albuquerque Opportunity Center seemed to understand. What was so difficult about the concept? The irony of course was that until it happened to me, I was clueless.

There was one other possibility, the community at large wanted nothing to do with me. It was fear. I wasn't some drugged out, crazed bum looking to mug them for my next fix. I had never been convicted of anything; hell the worst thing they could ever pin on me was a speeding ticket, in rural Nevada. So that was it! If it could happen to me, it could happen to them and they knew it. The economy was tanking, jobs were being lost. Most people didn't have large sums of money in the bank. What they did have was invested in their homes and they were always 90 days away from losing them if their income dried up or there was a family tragedy. I was symbolic of everything you don't want to think about because it turns your stomach into a writhing mass of butterflies that will not disperse without a hit of Xanax or a couple of drinks.

I was a living example of a problem they dare not consider. Nobody really shunned me, but not one person outside the homeless system or poverty medicine community ever tried to contact me, AND THAT INCLUDES MY ORIGINAL FAMILY, if only to wish me luck. I might as well not exist; I was the uninvited guest at the dinner table that everybody pretended wasn't there.

On the day before the surgery, my last meal at the mission, the preacher looked my way before diving into his sermon.

"Tomorrow, one of our own will pass through the valley of the shadow of death. Lord, be with him, comfort him, anoint his head with oil and see that his cup runneth over. This is a good man Lord, he's never hurt a soul. He's one of the children of Abraham, Isaac and Jacob. One of his ancestors was at Mount Sinai when you gave Moses the Ten Commandments. Please Lord, in the name of all that's holy, let him live — and maybe he'll come to Jesus – Amen."

Everybody laughed and more than a few "God Bless You's" were sent my way. I was toasted with cups of Lemonade and when the bus arrived to take us to back AOC, they made me sit up front, which was, I guess, a position of honor.

As the time came for lights out Billy came over and wished me well. He only had four days left at AOC, but he promised to visit me in the hospital and keep in touch, once I got out.

Sadly, I never saw or heard from him again!

The next morning I was awakened at 4:00 AM. The only way for me to get to the hospital was on the early morning van that took the day workers to their sweaty minimum wage jobs that began before the sunrise and sometimes ended after sunset.

As the Van climbed the hill towards the hospital, a piece of music (from my music school days) kept going though my head. It was called, "The Little Train of the Caipira" and was written by the great Brazilian composer Heiter Villa-Lobos. It told the story of a tiny steam engine that each day barely made its way to the top of a mountain so it could take the Caipira, the land workers to their jobs on the outskirts of the rain forest.

In my case, the van was carrying me to a new life or my last day on Earth. I had no idea which.

CHAPTER NINETEEN
Cabbage

The time has come, the Walrus said, to talk of many things,
Of shoes, of ships of sealing wax, of cabbages and kings.
—Lewis Carroll

I arrived at the University of New Mexico Hospital at 4:30 AM. There was nothing to do but wait, since preparation for the surgery wouldn't begin until 6:30 AM. Two hours, tick tock, two hours to what? They were going to open my chest and rip out my heart. Then find "harvesting sights," arteries I could spare to replace the ones that were blocked. One too many fried eggs, perhaps, but over a lifetime, who knows.

Lifetime, now there's a concept. My Grandfather lived to be 93, so did my Uncle Walter. Those were nice, ripe old ages, filled with accomplishments and wonders. Grandpa had gone from a world without electricity, into which he was born, to automobiles and airplanes. He lived to watch men land on the moon.

I was born into a world just recovering from a devastating war, radio was about to be replaced by television, and a great force, atomic energy, had been released, no one knew if for ultimate benefit or the destruction of the human species.

Before I was ten, they were building radar stations along the DEW line in Alaska and Northern Canada to keep an electromagnetic eye out for the

Soviet Bear Bombers that never came and most of which were never built. The cold war with its drop drills and wailing sirens were part of a hoax perpetuated by the US and the Soviets. When the moment came to hit the button during the Cuban Missile Crisis in 1962, everybody blinked. Even the evil bear Khrushchev didn't want to die with the death of millions on his conscience. But we, the kids, had the shit scared out of us with stories, songs and movies about a post apocalyptic world. On the beach, indeed.

I lived to see the space program unfold, the personal computer, new medications of every kith and kind, and perhaps most significantly the age of the Universe determined within a few hundred million years.

Tick. Tock.

There was a television in the waiting room tuned to CNN. I don't remember a single story. Time was passing very slowly, retarded by gravity, as though I were swirling towards my own personal event horizon beyond which lay the singularity we must all face, death itself. Would I miss the black hole and be shot off into space to live a little longer, or would I come to know that final enduring mysterious place and embrace it for eternity?

Tick. Tock.

A life started with so much promise: fame, fortune, accomplishment, now reduced to anonymity, grinding poverty, days and nights with nothing to do. I'd made the journey from yin to yang. A little boy with a bright world still ahead was now an aging man whose only hope of living lay in the hands of a surgical team, most of whom I would never meet.

"Mr. Barrett." A woman in green with a clipboard approached me. "It's time for your prep." Her voice was utterly unaffected by the seriousness of the moment.

"I'm ready." I said. Two words that summed up my life. No jokes, no attempt at charm, no vivacity, just utter resignation.

I gave up my clothing and possessions, slipped a thin cotton hospital gown over my naked body, but that was quickly removed so they could shave my chest. The last vestige of my hirsute masculinity was expertly removed by a man with an electric clipper.

For the first time I noticed that everybody was wearing surgical green. This was a no shit Sherlock group. A man with a cap covering his head sat down next to me. As he spoke, he removed an IV kit from its shrink wrapped package.

"Hello, Don, I'm your anesthesiologist Dr. Krauss. We'll only stick you once to put in your IV and then everything else will go into this little plastic petcock. We're going to give you something to relax and then I'll be back. I'm going to be by your side every minute of the surgery, checking your vital signs and administering anesthesia. Don't worry, you won't wake up and you won't remember anything."

As he said the last word I felt the stick of the needle, wincing only a little bit.

"I know you're scared, Don, but you have the best cardio team in the hospital and we're all here for one purpose: to get you through this."

I began to feel relaxed. I wanted to ask him if he had a joint so I could go out on a high, but of course, he wouldn't and I didn't. He got up and I was alone again. I closed my eyes since I was in a draped cubicle and there was nothing much to see. The only sound were the muffled conversations as prep teams moved from one patient to the next. Voices were low, there was no further information I could glean.

The front curtain on my cubicle slid open. Two men entered, one of whom was the anesthesiologist, his face now covered by a mask. He had a syringe which he did his best to keep out of my line of sight. The other man was there merely to wheel out my bed into the surgery.

"Okay Don, I'm going to ask you to slowly count backwards from 100 to zero."

"Tell Suzie Brin I was madly in love with her back in high school..." Perhaps my last confession on Planet Earth.

As the bed was expertly moved out of the prep area I could hear myself saying, "100, 99, 98..."

I never saw the surgical suite, the doctors or my 16 year old girlfriend again. I also never reached zero.

CHAPTER TWENTY
The Voice of the Turtle

The first thing I was aware of was a weight, not unlike a large SUV pressing down on my chest. I could feel the wiring that was holding my broken breast bone in a position so it could heal. When I first opened my eyes nothing registered. The room was dark, although there were lights blinking on the heart monitor, to which I was still attached. Every time it blinked it made a soft pinging sound which after a while (I don't know how long) became annoying. I was heavily bandaged and my range of motion limited, but I reached for the nurse's call button and pressed it.

Time was not something I could judge easily. I'm staring off into space without many thoughts going through my head. I felt certain my thinking was being inhibited by the huge cocktail of drugs I must have been given, but at this point I wasn't sure of anything.

"Mr. Barrett," it was the voice of a young woman. "I'm going to turn up the lights, if hurts your eyes just close them."

She did, and suddenly I felt I was looking directly into the sun's corona. I shut my eyes tightly and started to speak the word, "pain," but the only thing that came out was a rasping sound barely intelligible.

I took a deeper breath and tried again. It was a whisper. The nurse asked me, "Are you in pain? Just move your index finger and tap me once for yes."

With great effort I tapped.

"I'll ask the doctor to increase your pain meds. What else?"

"Voice." I whispered. There was no rasp or resonance to what had been a pretty decent speaking voice.

"That's not uncommon. A tube was placed down your throat to help you breath during surgery. Your voice will come back."

"When?" I whispered.

"Soon," was all she would say.

"If you want to watch television, I am putting the remote control into your left hand." She moved my hand around a remote video control, familiarizing me with the buttons and how to move the channels up and down. Three decades of television production and I'm reduced to this.

"Doctors will be by for grand rounds in about two hours. If you need anything before then call me with the nurse's button."

At that moment, all I wanted to do was lay there, staring into the returning darkness of the room. I had no roommate, which meant I was in the Cardio section of the hospital, 7th floor. I hurt, I couldn't talk, I felt fear of the unknown, the only positive emotion was that I was safe from mugging or assault, except by men and women who wielded scalpels and retractors. How long before I could recover or even walk again? What about my voice – it was part of the way I earned a living all my life, using my voice and command of the language to talk people into financing or distributing shows I was making or had made. Studio execs don't deal in the language of the deaf. Lingua con lingua mortua.

The studio. I flashed on a lunch held in the Executive Commissary at Paramount Pictures. I had been invited there to celebrate the release of the sequel to "Patrick Stewart narrates The Planets," "From Here to Infinity."

My host, Eric Doctorow, President of the Home Video Division and son of the writer was very charming and gracious. He seated me next to Howard Koch, the man who wrote (and adapted) "War of the Worlds" for Orson Welles. To my right was my producer, Robert H. Goodman, who'd formally been an agent with William Morris (now William Morris Endeavor – WME). I was right in the middle of two show business legends. If only my Grandfather could have seen me talking shop and answering questions about my inspiration for "From Here to Infinity."

"You're going to be a very successful man, Donnie, a producer or my God, a director." Thank you Aunt Yetta, for this moment in my life you were right. My name was up there on the screen, Written and Directed by Don Barrett. Is there some other dimension in which you know you were right?

My reverie was broken when a group of people entered the room. Many were wearing white, while others were in scrubs. One older man came forward, while a second intoned a whole series of observations and numbers from my chart. At this point I wasn't processing so it all sounded like gibberish to me. The older doctor looked at me, put his hand on my bandaged chest, saw me wince and ordered some morphine.

"Mr. Barrett, do you know where you are?"

"Hospital," I whispered.

"That's right. We operated on you, July 11th, replacing four arteries that were blocked and no longer carrying blood to your heart, with four unblocked arteries from your legs and your arms. You're heavily bandaged now, but you will have some scars."

"Women think that's sexy," I whispered reverting to humor to fight off the terror mode.

"And those women would be right." The doctor agreed. "You were on the table for 13 hours and spent three days in ICU. Today is July 14th and you're going to be our guest for a while. Starting tomorrow we're going to ask you to get up and walk. Now you may only get as far as the door, but each day you'll walk a little farther."

"My voice," I whispered, I wonder if he could hear the note of fear.

The doctor turned to one of his minions, "Let's schedule him for an ENT (Ear Nose and Throat) consult in a few days."

His attention returned to me. "We're going to keep you a bit sedated, your body has been through a lot, and I have to tell you there will be pain. We can't keep you at this level of pain killer forever and we'll gradually ease you off. Right now, we just want you to rest and begin the healing process."

He turned on his heel and followed the others back through the door. I was alone again. Being alone wasn't so bad, there were things I wanted to do but couldn't. Most of all I wanted to talk to my daughter Torrey, but without a voice we couldn't communicate. I wanted to insist her mother bring her to Albuquerque so I could see her face, but I knew that wouldn't happen. The level of hatred that Jackie felt for me, precluded even the smallest kindness. I'm sure, I was already dead in her mind.

Staring into the darkness couldn't go on forever, so I turned on the television. The first show that came on was "The Price is Right." I let its familiar cadences take over my mind. As nearly as I could suppose healing would be like fighting a war and, as General Theodore Roosevelt said at Omaha Beach on "D" day, June 6, 1944, "Well Marines, the war starts here."

CHAPTER TWENTY-ONE
The Unknown Nurse

For the next three days, I was mostly alone, and when I wasn't there was always a price to pay. Every four hours, as I had been warned, a nurse or a tech came in to give me a shot of Heparin. They introduced the shot different ways, "You're going to feel a pinch" or "This will only hurt for a second." The phrases were meant to keep me calm but none of them were true. It always hurt and hurt a lot. I decided I would never complain, because some little childish part of my mind was afraid they'd cut back on the pain meds.

Every time they'd give me a hit of pain medication, that SUV would be lifted from my chest, as though by a giant crane. Then slowly within an hour or so, it would return until the pain became unbearable, and I would be counting the minutes, the seconds until the next pain meds would be administered. That was the cycle of my life, the pain and the freedom from it.

Gradually, over a period of time, I was promised the pain would become less, but time takes on a special meaning when you're only a few days out of major surgery. It's almost impossible to think about next week or next month. Your mind is obsessed with getting through the next minute.

You must also understand that I was alone in a way few patients ever experience. Most people have families and when they are hospitalized, they receive visits. I was always good about going to the hospital to see relatives who had suffered heart attacks or surgeries, but I never really knew how welcomed those visits were; I didn't know how to read the look in the patient's eyes that carried their thanks for relief from the boredom of the pain cycle. Those visits also meant to the patients that somebody cared enough to stop by, regardless of the inconvenience or the weather. It meant somebody cared.

On the other hand, there was nobody who really cared for me – not the way a family member does. That would change but I don't want to get ahead of my story. In those first few days, I might as well have been trapped in the zone of silence, an especially empty part of East Antarctica. Other than the techs taking my blood, or the nurses reading my vitals or bringing medication, there was no connection between me and the rest of the human world. For reasons of sanitation, they always wore these awful purple latex gloves. The feeling of latex is not the same as human skin. It has an alien texture; it was almost like being touched by a robot. Intellectually, I could comprehend the reason, but emotionally it made me feel distant, not a real person, rather a thing that had to be treated but with a buffer always between it and the caregiver.

I began to think long and hard about all the times in my life I had touched people – I don't mean spiritually, but physically. Old girlfriends came to mind, even my ex-wife; it was as though my memory contained information about what their skin felt like, how it smelled, how it tasted when I kissed it and how everyone was different. What made me so sad was the thought that I didn't know if I would ever touch anybody that way again. Would I ever make love to a woman? Would I ever feel the softness of her cheek on the back of my hand. Was I now disconnected from the human race? Had I become a race of my own, Homo Patientus? What of the future – that nagging question I could never dismiss, that hung in their air like stale cigarette smoke: what would become of me?

On the third day since I had awakened, the room was dark. I assume it was early evening since I hadn't been given any of my evening's medication. The door cracked open but the light didn't come on. I could see the outline of a woman. She was slim, had long hair and as nearly as I could tell was wearing nursing scrubs, although I didn't know what her position in the hospital could be.

I started to talk, but she held a finger up to her mouth to silence me. Just as well, I had nothing to say. Then I noticed she didn't not reach for the latex gloves that were kept in a dispenser near the bed. She reached out her bare hand, and took mine in it. With her other hand she placed it on top and softly stroked the hand. At first she didn't say a word; she didn't need to. I felt an electric moment of connection, although I didn't know with whom. I felt tears running down my cheeks, not from pain, but from relief. Then she bent down and whispered in my ear, in the softest, most musical voice I can remember hearing, "You're going to be alright Don. I promise it."

After a few moments she put my hand back down on the bed, turned and left the room as quietly as she'd come. Who was this woman? Was she an angel of mercy, or just perhaps someone who knew how dire my situation was and how badly I felt. I will never know; I never saw her again, nor have I discussed the experience until writing this book, but I trace the beginning of my recovery from the surgery to that visit.

My guess is like any institution, there are few secrets in a hospital. I hadn't had any visitors or phone calls from family – that info would find its way onto my chart. In addition, the Shelter would be an emergency contact, so it wouldn't be too hard to figure out I was homeless. One of the nurses or techs, put two and two together and figured that I was bad-off, psychologically speaking, and needed some cheering up, in a way that doesn't conform to the standard medical protocols.

Somebody decided perhaps to take their break time and pay me a visit, if for no other reason to let me know they and the other members of my team cared. The fact is: she chose such a beautiful intimate way to pass that along. It could have been a more impersonal latex glove kind of patient interaction, but just like me, beating in this woman's chest was a heart, and in my opinion, a big one.

Whoever you are, wherever you are, you helped saved my life; you were there when I needed to be reminded that I, too, was human and though we've never really met, and I wouldn't recognize you if we passed in the halls, I want you to know that I love you and will never forget the few moments we spent together when you held my hand.

CHAPTER TWENTY-TWO
Perambulation

The next day brought with it the promise of a new adventure. A male nurse, the size of an NFL Linebacker cheerfully announced that it was time for me to walk. Honestly, with all my bandages, intravenous lines and heart monitor sensors I wasn't certain I could turn over, but no, they wanted me up and walking.

Surveying all of the hook-ups on me and deciding it was above his pay grade, the physical therapist called in one of the cardiac techs to unhook me. It was a methodical process that took about ten minutes and left me with a "tail" a circuit box that was still hooked up to me and dangled enough wires that Dr. Frankenstein would have had a drug free erection.

Of course, I was wearing the traditional hospital gown with its massive rear ventilation.

"Are you sure you want me to walk outside with my ass exposed?" I asked.

"Believe me," the PT replied, we've got nothing but little old ladies on this corridor. It'll be the highlight of their day. Just don't take any offense if they whistle at you."

The PT took me by the arm and helped me into a walker. If there's one device we associate with old age and even senility it's a walker. Believe me when I tell you there isn't a healthy 20, 30, or 40 year old in the country that puts "a walker" at the top of their Christmas list.

The first day, I barely made it to the door, before I was huffing and puffing as though I'd just climbed the Earth Mother of the World, Mt. Everest, Chungalungma. I couldn't seem to get enough oxygen in my lungs and I felt weak, dizzy and ready to collapse.

The PT didn't look upon this as utter failure. "Tomorrow we'll make it out the door. You'll see. For now, we'll just get you back into bed so they know where to find you when it's time for your Heparin shot."

"What a lovely thought." At this point I was sure that my stomach muscles had more holes in it than a Swiss cheese from the damn Heparin.

So carefully we put my exhausted body back into bed, found a comfortable position, and then buzzed for the cardio tech, so I could be wired back up like Robbie the Robot. I noticed that almost every time I was rewired, some contact was out of sequence and nursing rushed in when my cardiac alarm went off, as though my heart had caught fire.

Then I had another boring day to look forward to, mostly watching basic cable. Having spent a life in television I had no idea how bad daytime TV was or how obnoxious commercials had become.

For one thing, the networks had given up the hard news to the cable news outlets. As far as The Today Show and Good Morning America were concerned, the state of the economy, or the imminent chances of war were of less importance then an exclusive interview with the mistress of a humiliated Presidential contender. This was journalism right off the rack at the Smiths supermarket. I can only assume that with more and more intelligent women going to important jobs, the only people left to watch this crap were women who would never get out of the house and the men they tortured.

Quickly burning out on news I turned to the game shows for a little brain stimulation. I rather enjoyed the giveaway shows because it was nice to see the happy smiles on the faces of the people who had waited in line all night and won a new stripped down 2007 Ford Forget It. They jumped in the air, screamed with abandon, and then went and caressed their new low end automobile as though it were a BMW 750i. Whatever, they could always sell it for $12,000 and then after paying taxes on their winnings, buy a four year old Hyundai.

Other than Jeopardy with its totally obscure questions like: name three science fiction operas ("Aniara," "The Markopoulos Affair" and "Help Help The Globolinks") most asked questions that reasonably educated people should know, but obviously some don't. For instance, on one show a recent UCLA graduate was asked "How many states are there in the lower 48?" Her response was, "Does that include Alaska and Hawaii?"

Okay so I know I'm smarter than a fifth grader although I'm willing to bet not many ten year old kids, with names like Molokai, Muleteer and Desdemona would know the distance of a furlong (1/8th of a mile). Still they held back the most difficult fifth grade question for the bonus: "In the 14th century BC, what was the prevailing language of New Zealand?" I'm sure every kid knows that that the Maori hadn't settled New Zealand 3400 years ago, but of course the contestant didn't. Then to add insult to injury these poor schlubs had to look into the camera and declare they were not smarter than a fifth grader. A fifth grader where? The Einstein School for Little Geniuses? Oh Mark Burnett you devil!

The truth is, in my heart or hearts, I think I'm smarter than Judge Judy ("On the smartest day of your life, you're not as smart as I am on the dumbest day of mine.") Oh really, Judy? What's the largest known star in the Milky Way? Come on Judith? VY Canis Majoris, you fail today's smart test Judge, it's the showers for you.

But as diverting as television might have been, it couldn't break the pain cycle. To lessen my frustration with it, they provided me with a device that allowed me to inject a little pain killer into my IV. Believe me, it was like pouring a drop of water on the Chicago Fire. I hurt plenty but every time I'd ask for more medication, they'd say, "We have to be very careful about that. We don't want you to become addicted."

I reminded them that numerous studies had shown that addiction comes from using drugs recreationally when you don't have pain, but it didn't do any good. They kept reminding me, they were the experts and I was nothing more than a patient (which I suppose comes from the word patience – meaning you should be able to wait forever for your pain meds).

Later that afternoon, I was in for a wonderful surprise. Shannon, from AOC brought her mother Bren, and I actually had visitors. I was so grateful for their caring enough about me to stop by. I must have looked a sight what with all the lines going in and out, but they never said anything about it.

Shannon reported that the respite bed area was under construction and they were saving the best bed for me. Bren also brought me a book to read, which was a damn sight more stimulating that anything on basic cable. Considering my condition they couldn't stay very long, but they were like a shot in the arm of medication that the hospital's pharmacy didn't stock. For a little while anyway, I felt pretty good and not so lonely. Then the pain hit again and I begged the nurse for something that would put me to sleep. I was tired of fighting it eighteen hours a day. After an hour she got permission to give me an Ambien but promised to wake me in four hours with yet another shot of Heparin. Sometimes, a bad deal is better than no deal, so I agreed, took the Ambien and waited for my date with the blackness of somnolence, knowing it would end with a prick in the stomach.

CHAPTER TWENTY-THREE
Vocalize

How exciting! The past three days I have ventured further and further into the hallway, holding desperately onto my walker. I know my ass was the talk of 7th floor, but how much can you say about a 60 year old butt? ("It doesn't sag as much as I thought it would?")

I have to assume everybody else on the cardiac floor was as bored as I, since every day, during my walk, I ran into the same 85 year old lady, who had the good sense to wear a pink bathrobe. No free peaks at her derriere! She smiled at me but we never exchanged a word.

Today I got as far as the first nurses' station and then turned around and headed for the barn. Arriving at my bed I felt I had just done a 4.3 second forty yard dash for the NFL Combine. I rang for the tech to hook me up again, but instead was met by a dashing woman holding a wheel chair.

"Hello, I'm Maggie, the speech therapist. We're going downstairs and take a peak at your throat, to see why you haven't got your voice back. Care to join me?"

I would have preferred joining her in a hot tub, but the wheel chair was padded and we had a refreshing conversation, considering I had to whisper all the way down to four east.

"So what do you do Mr. ....Barrett?" she read from the file.

"Believe it or not," I rasped, "I'm a writer, producer and director in film and television."

"So what are you doing in Albuquerque?"

She must have known that damn Promotion Manager, who hadn't called me once since I'd been in the hospital, but then neither had my ex-wife, or my daughter. Oh, the brainwashing that child must have been receiving. How do you not call your Dad, who's suffered a heart attack and life threatening surgery. My God, she must hate me. Will she ever love me again?

Thank goodness my cogitation was brought to an end as we entered four east, the Speech Therapy Center. I met the surgeon and he looked young enough to date my daughter, and if he did, I'd get him for statutory.

"Well, Mr. Barrett. Your voice still hasn't returned to normal?"

"No," I whispered, "that's why I'm here." I was never this cocky on the street. All this attention had me feeling my oats.

"How about we look down your throat?" he asked. I expected him to pull out one of those popsicle sticks and ask me to say "Ah."

Instead he had a thick, fiber optic camera with a built in light that he was going to slip down my throat. On the first try I started to gag, and spit bile all over his clean white coat. So the next time, he took a small cotton bandage and grabbed ahold of my tongue and started pulling, as though it were an endless roll of toilet paper and he could pull forever. All that was left for me was to grunt, as he cleverly slipped his camera past my tongue to my larynx. Unfortunately, his new, but very attractive assistant, Maggie the Oaf, had forgotten to record this, so we had to do it all over.

Now all I had to do was make a sound before I puked again. I tried, but nothing came out. The voice of the turtle was not heard in the Speech Therapy Center.

He played back a video recording of my larynx on a monitor and showed me that it wasn't moving.

"I'm afraid it's paralyzed," he said, "must have happened during the intubation."

I whispered closely into his ear, "In many ways I earn a living with my voice."

"Oh are you a singer?" He asked querulously.

"No, I'm a director and a producer. I tend to do a lot of talking."

"Well, not for a while." He made it sound like a joke but I failed to find anything funny in the end of my career, such as it was.

"I don't mean to frighten you, Mr. Barrett. There is an implant surgery that can fix this problem most of the time, but it will be months before you're healthy enough for that procedure. I should tell you, though, it's not a pleasant operation, since you'll be awake the entire time."

"Why is that?" I wondered quietly.

"So that when we've finished you can make a sound that will tell us if we got it right, or if you'll be the next Marcel Marceau."

He was dating himself, but maybe that was the best he could do. Oh lovely, I thought, the whole operation was an experiment. Just what I needed, but if it would give me my voice back...

"We'll schedule up something for about three months from now and we'll check your larynx every month, until then."

What a joy, I'm going to be good friends with a tongue puller and his thick-as-a-redwood-tree fiber optic camera.

"Can't you get a thinner camera," I asked, "like the spies use?"

"There is a thinner model set to come out next year. It's an expensive little bugger. Miss Wheeler (honest - that was her name) would you take Mr. Barrett back to his room?"

"Yes, Doctor."

"See you in a month, Mr. Barrett."

"Can't wait!" I rasped back.

Miss Wheeler took up the conversation. "Wasn't that exciting seeing your larynx on television?"

"A thrill, better than the Thanksgiving Show I did with Loretta Switt."
"Who?" Asked the recent graduate of the You Too Can Have a Trade University.

"Loretta Switt, MASH." I whispered.

"No, I prefer boiled potatoes." She rejoined and the ride up the elevator seemed to take a lifetime.

CHAPTER TWENTY-FOUR
Shrink Wrapped

Ten days had gone by; that's a lifetime in an acute care hospital, where they have to account daily for a reason why you're taking up a valuable bed on the cardio floor. In other words, if they discharge you today, will you die, or just feel like shit?

After the usual rounds, a young man came in wearing a full length white coat, but without a stethoscope draped around the back of his neck. In a place where everybody was draped he looked almost undressed.

"Hello, I'm Dr. Welcome (honest), a behavioral therapist."

"Is that a polite name for a psychiatrist?" I inquired.

"That's a good guess, I wish I had a prize to offer."

"Conversation has been a scarce commodity around here, Doctor. Let's consider that the prize." I whispered.

"It's a deal. You've had it pretty rough, Mr. Barrett, based on what your chart tells me." He sat down and elegantly folded one leg over the other.

"Do you know it all?" I whispered, my voice still not having come back a whit.

"I know you were homeless following a divorce. You tried committing suicide with a plastic knife."

"Pretty pathetic, don't you think, Doctor."

"I've seen worse. To continue you've suffered a heart attack and a quadruple bypass. You've only had two visitors, so I guess you're pretty much a stranger in Albuquerque."

Even the good Doctor (I've got your chart and know everything about you) didn't have a clue about my five minutes with the unknown nurse nor would he find out from me, not a whisper.

"Yes, a stranger in a strange land, to quote the Bible and author Robert Heinlein."

"So Mr. Barrett, how do you feel going back to the shelter to recover. It may take months, you know."

"As long as I don't have to go back on the street. That would be grounds for switching from a plastic knife to something more effective."

"I don't see that happening, but I'll make a notation on your chart. The shelter doesn't want to see you fail. You're intelligent, you will be articulate once we take care of your larynx, so there's no reason you can't go back to a normal life. You might even find a lady to your liking." He was offering me hope when I was hopeless.

"Well, Doctor, for the right lady I could summon a modicum of charm, but I have to find work. I understand that when all is said and done I'll be eligible for $635 a month in state disability. That's going to limit my potential for a hot date or even one that's scarcely breathing."

"Yes, well, there are problems you'll have to solve. My point is, as long as you maintain your health, you have the capability of resolving them. Once again, the world could be your Oyster, unless you keep Kosher, that is."

"Keeping Kosher on the street isn't easy or even possible. I am interested in the future, even though the one that I see is mired in the haze."

"I'm very glad to hear that Mr. Barrett, because in a couple of days, you'll be going – well I can't really call it home – but it's the next best thing."

"It scares the hell out of me, Doctor. I feel safe and except for the pain, reasonably comfortable here. Once I leave I have to restrain my personality once again and adapt. I want my voice back so I can talk about what I've been through and what I've seen. I would like to be an advocate for the homeless or at least a voice in the wilderness. I want the rest of America to know what it's like being a non-person."

He stood and surveyed the room, "Well you may get your chance, but first you have a lot of recovery ahead of you. It may be years before you're ready to talk about your experience and then it's possible you may never want to discuss it with anyone. There's a lot of embarrassment attached to failing in life and becoming homeless, especially when one has fallen from a pretty lofty position. Oh yes, Mr. Barrett, I know who you are. I have three of your videos at home. I was a teenager when my mother gave me, 'Patrick Stewart narrates The Planets' and I nearly wore it out. I have the feeling if anyone can come back it will be you. Just don't expect a smooth path. Life will remain unpredictable, and you'll have to roll with the punches."

"I suppose that's an exit line." I said to the man in white.
"I have other patients. Good luck, Sir, try to remember the quote you put in Patrick Stewart's mouth at the end of the video."

"Yes, the one from J.B.S. Haldane: 'The Universe isn't merely more than we imagine, it's more than we can imagine.'"

"Now that, Don Barrett, is an exit line."

CHAPTER TWENTY-FIVE
Theme from The New World Symphony
Or
Going Home

Well what can you say when your home is a homeless shelter? The answer is: it's better than the street.

Two days after my visit with the head shrinker, an announcement came with my breakfast. I was being discharged after spending 12 days in the hospital. The process, I learned, is slow and grinding. Basically, everyone in the world has to sign off, medical prescriptions are filled, checked, double checked, all that paper work passes through administration, while you wait and wait.

I got so desperate I started watching Soap Operas. Finally, I understand why the young are so restless. They just want to get the damn show over with. Now I don't want to sound like a total soap opera snob. I remember following grandmother around the house, when I was too young to go to school. She had a radio in every room so not a moment of the morning line-up on CBS would be missed as she cleaned. I got to know "Ma Perkins," "The Romance of Helen Trent" and, of course, "Our Gal Sunday." Helen Trent was the worst. For thirty years she proved, "…as so many women long to prove in their own lives: that because a woman is 35 romance in life need not be over. That romance can continue to 35 and even beyond." By the time the show went off the air, ageless Helen Trent must have been 65 and still running after that no good carouser Gil Whitney, a lawyer with a wandering eye—I got the impression that all it did was wander – this was the late 1940's after all.

But I digress, after waiting about six hours to check out I finally get a call that the van from the shelter was waiting for me and a wheel chair to add to my humiliation was on the way. At least I was free of those dangling wires, although I was still heavily bandaged. Those would come off in a few days, and most of my follow-up care would be through Healthcare for the Homeless, a truly wonderful institution that practiced poverty medicine at its most basic level.

Anyway, in comes a tech with a wheel chair and we take the elevator down to a shady little grotto where Shannon and the Van are waiting for me.

"How are you," Shannon asked in her effusive manner.

"I'm alive, now you've got to keep me that way."

"Oh don't you worry, wait until you see how we've fixed the place up. You have a new bed, mattress, a chest of drawers donated by the Thrift Shop on Menaul, real pajamas, a bathrobe, slippers, books; they've completely walled off the new respite care beds. Oh and you have two roommates, nice guys, Darrell and Dale."

Okay, so I would be in close quarters with two guys I didn't know, but hopefully we'd all get along. Right now, I needed some rest. Doing the smallest task was exhausting. The pain in my breast bone had subsided a little, it only hurt badly when I breathed in.

I really wasn't prepared for the greeting I received when we arrived at the shelter. The evening bus from the mission had already brought in most of the residents, and they practically formed a line shaking my hands, giving me high fives, and clapping me on the back. Apparently, the guys mistook me for some kind of hero, something in rather short supply on the streets. I felt a little dazed by all the attention, although I noticed Shannon standing off to the side with a big smile on her face – I couldn't help but feel she had something to do with this giant morale booster. You know, however, the good feelings worked two ways; for me it was obvious, who wouldn't get pumped up by this kind of greeting, but for the men, to see one of their own survive what would have been a sure fatality on the streets, must have made them feel collectively that somebody was looking out for them too. If I, an out of shape 60 year old could survive a heart attack and quadruple bypass, then each of them had a damn good chance as well. In other words, the loss of their health was no longer a death sentence, although it would have been for me without the intervention of AOC and I was later to learn, other agencies that had cooperated in the respite program.

Once the big hello was over, Shannon escorted me over to the new respite area which had one high wall dividing it from the main dormitory and a shorter wall that cut it off from the TV lounge area. That would become a minor issue later on, since there were guys who wanted to watch TV all night, and that didn't sit well with the three of us on respite who were all out of the hospital and needed our sleep.

My roommates were a couple of real interesting characters. Hyperkinetic Dale always seemed to be moving in four directions at once. He talked fifty miles an hour, but to his credit he was always trying to do everything for everyone. Dale suffered from Epilepsy, and was subject to Grand Mal seizures (the worst kind). He was crossing the street when suddenly an electrical storm broke out in his brain and he went down on the ground uncontrollably seizing. Some driver wasn't paying attention to the homeless guy and ran him over, severely injuring his left arm. The driver didn't bother to stop or Dale might have had the benefit of some insurance protection. Some kinder soul found him on the ground still in a seizure and called 911. The paramedics found him in a post-seizure trance with a bone sticking out of his arm. The docs at UNMH screwed it back into place, but apparently didn't do a great job, because you could almost see a screw coming out of his wound.

I tried to help him get a lawyer who did malpractice, but none of the guys who advertised on daytime television would take the case. So Dale healed as best he could and swallowed pain pills by the handful.

Darrell was a laid back good old boy, with red hair and a matching mustache. For most of his life he'd been a roughneck, an oil worker, who hung out on the fourble boards of Southern New Mexico, breaking down thribbles of pipe. Tough dirty work though it was, I never heard him complain about it. He'd spent most of his life around the oil rigs near Lovington, New Mexico, working his ass off during the days and chasing away the dirt and smell of the oil with a few well placed beers in the evening. He was married until his wife died, and soon thereafter his mother passed as well. At that point, Darrell became disinterested in his life, began to drift around, went through his money and ended up on the street. He didn't look it but he was a tough son of a bitch, until he suffered an embolism in his leg, which was part of a general circulatory problem. The pain was awful, and Darrell got badly hung up on the medication, not that I'll ever blame someone who eats Oxycodone and is in real pain.

The trouble was the doctors would only prescribe him twenty pills at a time which he could go through in one day. The next day he'd be sitting watching a movie on television and this tough guy would have tears rolling down his cheeks and they weren't the sentimental kind from watching Rocky V. His problem was pretty much chronic – there didn't seem to be anyway out for Darrell. A couple of times, my own pain meds disappeared until I made sure to lock them up. They nearly put him on the street for that, but I kind of begged them to forget – I wasn't going to complain as long as it didn't happen again. Darrell was the sort of guy you wanted to slip an extra Vicodin, except with the kind of pain he suffered he'd never notice the narcotic effect. For Darrell the grinding pain was always there – I don't know how he stood it.

My first night back at the shelter I slept like the dead. I didn't hear the guys being awakened at 5:30 to get dressed so they could eat at the Mission by 6:00. When I finally did awaken, I did not feel rested. It was a monumental effort to make it to the rest room and back, my version of a marathon. I just kept taking my medication, hoping that it would get better. I couldn't help but think about what the doc had said about the road ahead not being easy. I didn't expect I would recover like I'd just suffered a mild case of the flu, but I had no idea of what bumps might lay ahead.

According to Shannon, it was about 4:00 on the afternoon of my second day that she heard a pounding on the door to the upstairs office. It was Dale, who was so excited he could hardly talk. Instead he pointed to my bed in the respite area. As Shannon came down the stairs she could see I wasn't in it.

I was lying face down on the floor and she couldn't tell if I were dead or alive.

CHAPTER TWENTY-SIX
City of Eternal Night

Blackness. I was a captive of the City of Eternal Night. I can remember no thought passing through my mind, no emotion, no fear. People have asked me if I saw a white light drawing me ahead, or had a vision of God, the truth is: I don't know. Whatever I saw or felt was erased from my memory.

I don't remember the paramedics screaming at me, looking for some sign of recognition, nor being loaded into the ambulance. I don't recall the shock of the defibrillation paddles, entering the emergency room, being hooked up once again to the heart monitors. The only hazy memory, I'm not even sure it's an accurate one, was lying in the darkness wondering if I was going to join all the billions that had lived and died.

When I awoke, it was in a hospital bed, but not on the cardio floor this time. Across an expanse of curtain, lay another man, moaning. I could hear voices, probably relatives of my roommate speculating if this was the end. It was. I recall them taking his body out and wondering if I would have company once again, for there was nobody standing by me. I could now hear only the sound of my breathing accompanied by the beep of the heart monitor. What had happened? I thought my heart problems were behind me. I had new arteries, with no plaque, nothing to stop the river of blood. I was alive or was I dead?

With all my strength I reached for the nurse call and pushed the button. After what seemed like an eternity, a stout woman with a friendly smile came into the room and over to my bed. She reset the nurse call and asked me what I needed.

"What happened?" I asked.

"I don't know. You were brought here. Your doctor will be by in the morning to explain everything. Right now I suggest you sleep."

"You won't tell me?"

"I don't know," was all she would say. She turned and left the room and all I had to keep me company was endless speculation.

I tossed and turned as much as the IV's and electrical wiring would permit. After half an hour I called the nurse again and requested some sleep medication, which had been prescribed but for some reason not administered. I drifted off to sleep, my life a question mark. I wondered if my slumber would be interrupted by a shot of Heparin, but it wasn't.

I awoke at 6:00 as the tech was getting my vitals for the chart. I didn't expect the tech knew or would say anymore than the nurse did last night, so I didn't bother to ask. I didn't feel much like talking or rather whispering anyway. I had some questions that I knew wouldn't be answered for an hour or more, there was no point muchering over the subject, like a mouse over a crumb of cheese.

The Today Show is a distraction, although the women's fashion segments bore the hell out of me. At last, the doctors and nurses who have been appointed to do Grand Rounds enter my room. They look uncomfortable and mumble a great deal. Finally, one of the older doctors approaches me.

"How are you feeling, Mr. Barrett?" He asks.

"Very confused. What exactly am I doing here?"

"Well," he hesitates, "There was an anomaly in your recuperation."

"Can you tell me exactly what that means, please Doctor?"

"We don't know exactly. When the paramedics arrived your heart was not beating, but subsequent to their intervention it has been functioning normally. It's possible you had an allergic reaction to the combination of medication."

"Isn't that something you test for, before you issue the prescriptions?" I wonder if my voice is capable of carrying irritation – I doubt it.

"Tests are never 100% accurate, Mr. Barrett. We are very sorry for the inconvenience."

"I'd hardly think my brush with death as a mere inconvenience." I'm actually thinking lawyer at this point, but I'm not about to say anything. "So, where do we go from here?"

"We're going to keep you a few days to stabilize and observe you. We'll make certain there is no repetition."

"I sincerely hope not, after all, how many times does a man have to die in one lifetime!"

There was a small titter of laughter, nervous laughter, the kind of laughter suffixed with "You do not pay a dime unless we get you an insurance award." The doctor squeezed my arm (seems to be a regular practice) and the group departed. So, once again I was ushered to the portals of Hades, this time by a bad mixture of medicine. I felt like a deflated balloon. I was back to square one. I'd survived delicate life threatening surgery and now I was back in the hospital, nearly killed by the very medicine that was suppose to protect me.

I felt completely out of control. What more did I have to do to prove myself worthiness of life?

Damn it, this wasn't fair. I did everything I was supposed to, I'd made it through twelve days of unrelenting scrutiny, I achieved freedom making it back to the shelter for recovery and without doing a thing, here I was back in the hospital, with no idea how many return trips I'd be making.

All those years of never having lain in a hospital bed meant nothing. Where could I find any security in life? I was destitute, sick and homeless. To what could I look forward? Men my age were already playing with their grandchildren. Torrey, thank God, wasn't having any babies yet, but her time would come and would I be part of her life? Would I even be alive to watch another generation come of age with a little of my DNA? The questions were overwhelming, and there were no answers. I felt like a fly caught in amber, unable to move forward in space or time; my identity slipping away. What had happened to a life so full of promise? The same question turned over and over like an old fashioned needle on a broken record: what dear God would become of me?

CHAPTER TWENTY-SEVEN
The Phrygian Mode

Do you know what's missing from a hospital? Music. All my life music has played an important role in my emotions. Even as a preteen adolescent I would spend hours in my room, letting music play with my emotions, absorbing new creative energy from the sound. Of all the languages on planet Earth, none is like music. It requires no phonemes, nor does it need to be translated. In some form or another, we find music in every culture from the ancient Coroboree of the Australian Aborigine to the most sophisticated atonal extra musical creations of 20th Century America and Europe – I'm thinking Concerto for Airplane and Orchestra.

Music, no matter its age, always exists in the now, whether in performance or the mind of the listener. Hospitals are one place that put very little stock in the power of music to uplift and maybe to heal.

When my daughter was still inside the womb, the ob-gyn attending my wife, suggested I put together a tape of soothing and beautiful music to be played during the stage of labor that precedes childbirth. He thought it would be good for Jackie. I put a lifetime of musical knowledge into that tape. I wanted to create precisely the emotional state that would be most conducive to childbearing, although I admit I didn't and don't know precisely what that is. My daughter Torrey was born to "The Dance of the Sugar Plumb Fairy" from the "Nutcracker Suite." In fact, at the moment she crowned the tinkle bell sound of the Celeste is first heard. For some reason, I don't think it was all that coincidental.

Now as I lay in the hospital bed, with no tape or compact disc player available, I began forming music inside my head. Again, I don't believe it was coincidence, that the music which came to me was the "Fantasia on a Theme of Thomas Tallis" by my favorite composer, the Englishman, Ralph Vaughan Williams. The Tallis Fantasia is one of his most remarkable works, and considering he was in the top ten composers of the 20th century that gives it quite a distinction. In it, Vaughan Williams turns two string orchestras and a separate string quartet into the sound of the greatest pipe organ ever conceived by a musical brain.

The music doesn't just present itself on a two dimensional stage, but flows from all around you, engulfs your brain, lifts your spirit to a plane not of this world. If God has a theme, it must surely be this. Written in the Phrygian mode, there were modes before there were keys, it is sound driven to its maximum achievement; that of wordless communication of ideas and concept which have no name, but are felt at the most visceral level.

It is the most passionate music I've ever heard. My uncle, the film composer once told me that everything creative is about emotion. A movie, play or music devoid of emotion has nothing to offer. I believe he was right. Without benefit of anything but my musical memory I let the Tallis Fantasia wash over me. I no longer felt helpless or damned, but rather part of some larger consciousness that maybe you can only reach, when your life has been driven to the edge. More importantly, while the music pulsed through my mind I was no longer scared.

While I found comfort in this musical thrall, there was a war going on around me that I only became aware of when I received a phone call from Shannon on the third day of my return stay.

"How are you feeling?" She asked.

I rasped, "I want to get out of here. When can I go back to the shelter."

She hesitated. "There are problems. They're afraid to take you back. Everyone is freaked out at what happened."

"Shannon, I have nowhere to go. They won't keep me here forever, it's way too expensive, and according to what they tell me, there's no place for me to recover."

"I know, Don. I think the hospital has to assure the Board of Directors that this isn't going to happen again. We're not equipped, the program was never designed for respite care patients nearly dying on us." She was starting to cry, this was hard for her to tell me and I'm not sure the shelter would have been pleased.

"I need to talk to my doctors and the hospital administrator. They have to provide AOC with whatever will make its management feel comfortable taking me back. I'll really die on the street, but in this case it would be an act of murder."

"We'll talk later." She said.

"I have to get pro-active. I have to be my own advocate." I hung up the phone and began to plan my strategy. Sick as I was, I wasn't helpless. I still had my brain and as long as I did, I was a formidable adversary for administrators, doctors, lawyers, whatever. I had to talk my way back to the only place that would have me. The real question in my mind was would they listen?

I hit the nurse's call button and in about five minutes the floor nurse entered the room.

"We have a situation," I began, "I'd like to speak to the hospital's administrator as soon as possible."

"Mr. Barrett, the administrator is a busy man, is there anything I can do?"

"I'm afraid the problem is above your pay grade and you really don't want to be in the middle. Please tell the administrator that if I don't get some sort of response in the next hour, I'll be calling local television and the press. Have him check my file and see why I'm in here and I'm sure he'll want to give this his personal attention."

I was going to be firm but polite, my experience being this approach gets more done than going ballistic.

"I'll see what I can do." She said with considerable hesitation, but I had no doubt a call would be made, and when the hospital was looking at a potential malpractice lawsuit, that exceeded the national debt, there would be some sort of response.

Less than an hour later, three men and a woman entered my room. They were all neatly dressed in business attire. The woman had a legal air about her. Having been married to a lawyer for nearly twenty years, I could sense it.

"We understand there's a problem, Mr. Barrett. How can we assist you?" The oldest of the group, a white haired gentleman who smacked of prestige was going to the be the spokesperson, he was either the administrator or lead counsel for the hospital. I could deal with that.

"With whom am I speaking?" I asked.

"I'm an assistant administrator of this institution. Our administrator is out of town at a conference."

I explained the situation in a calm measured cadence, although I was still reduced to a whisper. I was here because of some mistake in my medication. Furthermore I was homeless and now the one place I could recuperate was reluctant to accept me without the assurance that my near death experience wasn't going to recur.

"It's like this," I said, "I've been put in an untenable position and I need your intervention."

"Are you looking for some kind of medical guarantee, Mr. Barrett? That would be difficult for us to provide." He said in a careful tone.

"I think it would be appropriate for you to contact the Executive Director at the Albuquerque Opportunity Center and determine his requirements. I'm sure they are quite reasonable, as are the organization's concerns. I think in light of the circumstances, you also have an obligation to see that my recovery not be impeded by a lack of mutual understanding between the parties."

The lawyer gave me a look. I expect he didn't think homeless people could speak beyond single syllables, in my case a whisper, a complete sentence, much less sound like they had participated in the Harvard Negotiation Project.

He tapped the Assistant Administrator on the shoulder and took over the conversation. "I'm the chief legal counsel for the hospital, Mr. Barrett. We'll contact the executive director and do our best to work out something mutually acceptable. In the meantime may we have your assurance that you won't air this matter in a public forum?" He was taking me seriously, good.

"As a matter of good will counselor, I will aver for the time being, but I'd like to be kept in the loop. Please advise me once you've talked to Mr. Plummer."

"We'll do that, Mr. Barrett and thank you for your cooperation."

"Thank you, Counselor, please understand, in addition to their liability concerns, I believe AOC has my best interest in mind."

The group nodded and walked out of the room. For a moment I felt like a Philadelphia lawyer that just won his first case, but I knew there would be some back and forth negotiation. I was holding the ace; they didn't want me appearing on the news, telling this story from my point of view, even if their surgeons had saved my life.

Several hours later the lead counsel reappeared to inform me that the matter had been solved. I was going to spend two more days stabilizing and then I'd return to the shelter. Once again I thanked him for his effort. As he turned to leave he smiled my way.

"You know Mr. Barrett, you should have studied law."

"In a way I did sir, for almost twenty years. My former wife was a graduate of Dartmouth and Harvard Law."

He sighed and left the room. After one defeat after another I'd won a not so small victory. The question that still hung in the air was now would I recover at AOC or play a return engagement at the hospital?

CHAPTER TWENTY-EIGHT
Dream a Little Dream of Me

I never wanted to be an actor, though there was some encouragement thrown my way. What I did want was recognition for something, call it applause, no make that cheers, the unspoken desire was the source of many dreams while in the shelter. I've alluded to it earlier, but at the age of eight my Uncle Walter actually did something kind for me – probably at my mother's annoying insistence.

Walter had just finished making the movie, "Hans Christian Anderson" with Danny Kaye and the film was quite popular especially with children. It was shot in particularly vivid Technicolor and boasted some wonderful songs, "Inchworm," "Thumbelina" and "Copenhagen." As it turns out Walter wrote all the original music for the score and was rewarded with an Oscar nomination. It also began a long professional relationship with Danny Kaye.

Mr. Kaye was booked to perform at Hollywood Bowl, the world famous amphitheater, and he asked Walter to arrange the music and conduct the orchestra. It was my honor to sit in the pit with the musicians and watch. At the time, there was actually a moat that separated the stage from the audience, it was all part of the allure of the Bowl.

Well the first half of the concert was absolutely incredible. Danny sang, Danny danced, he even brought a little boy on stage with him, which the audience loved. At the end of the first act, he brought the house down with "Ugly Duckling" and the applause washed over the stage like a wave breaching

132

the shore. How much I wanted those applause to be for me. I closed my eyes and pretended I was on stage and the audience was celebrating a truly remarkable performance. It was like a drug, being loved by so many people, an incredible thrill for a lonely only child.

At the intermission, I was taken to the "Green Room" where I was to wait quietly while my uncle changed his tux; it's quite normal for a conductor to sweat through his clothes and change them half way through the show. So I sat with nothing to do, but listen to the din of the audience.

Suddenly a man with red hair appeared, of course it was Danny Kaye.

"...and whose little boy are you?" He asked.

"My uncle is conducting the orchestra." I replied respectfully.

"...and what a fine job he's doing. So what is your favorite song. I will sing it just for you!"

I knew a dozen Danny Kaye songs by heart, but my favorite was the impossible tongue twisting "Tchaikovsky" that had been written by Danny's wife, Sylvia Fine.

"You want me to sing 'Tchaikovsky'? Veh is Mir. (Woe is me!) Okay sit on my lap."

I obediently sat on Danny Kaye's lap while he rattled off the names of 56 Russian composers in sixty-one seconds and made it all rhyme. I was delighted, he gave me a big hug, and went on about his merry way. Imagine, one of the biggest stars in the world entertaining me, a nobody kid.

It was my second night back from my second stay in the hospital and I awoke to the sound of one hand clapping, which is to say I awoke to no sound at all.

CHAPTER TWENTY-NINE
Recovery

It was the morning of my third day back. I was very weak – just getting up to go to the bathroom was act of supreme will. I was sitting in a chair, eating a day old bagel that Einstein's had donated to the shelter. Suddenly the chair went one way and I went the other way. I fell, twisting my right foot. A red wave of unadulterated pain shot through me, my foot began to swell and I couldn't stand.

Shannon drove me over to Albuquerque's Healthcare for the Homeless, the wonderful institution that specializes in poverty medicine that I mentioned earlier. They took an x-ray and determined that a small bone in the foot was broken. The doc bandaged it as best he could, saying it didn't warrant a full cast, but I would have to stay off it for a while. They gave me a set of crutches, but honestly I've never had the best sense of balance and found it hard to motivate with them. Somebody dug up an old wheel chair which was so decrepit it had to be pushed by somebody. You couldn't make it go by moving the wheel. Now I was truly a pain in the ass.

Dale and Darrell came to the rescue though and whenever I needed pushing they were Johnny-on-the-spot to get me where I needed to go. Both men had a tough exterior, but beneath it were hearts that only wanted to help their fellow respite mate. I'd never hung out with anyone quite like them, but we became fast friends and one day we carved our names on a rock just outside the door to the respite facility. Don – Dale – Darrell 2007.

I spent a lot of time on my back and despite a surfeit of books I used those hours and days to reflect on my life and to think about the future. Except for the people with whom I worked, I was always distant from the audience. In 1985 I worked on the American Music Awards Show which garnered the largest number of viewers of any show I'd ever done – 43 million. My work was touching an unimaginable number of lives, but I was touching nobody.

It's impossible to imagine 43 million people. The largest crowd of which I'd ever been apart, had been at a football game at the Los Angeles Memorial Coliseum. The Rams were playing the 49ers and 103,000+ turned out for the big rivalry. I just remember a sea of humanity stretching almost from horizon to horizon (I was a short ten year old). Now this television show was being seen by 430 times as many people, living their lives in everything from mansions to trailer parks; their situations were beyond my ability to imagine. What were they doing? What where they thinking? Was I, Don Barrett, having some kind of affect on them?

Perhaps I was part of an entertainment, a distraction from the daily grind of their lives, but little else. In the great department store of life, I was the toy section. My grandparents were wrong. Entertainment was not the highest calling, but it was the only calling I really knew. It would be up to me to figure out a way to make some kind of difference, if I ever got out of this place.

Slowly, and I do mean slowly, my foot began to heal and I hobbled my way around the shelter, talking to people, letting them know what had happened to me, and that as long as they had their health, they could make their way out of homelessness and live a better life. Before long people would come to me to ask how I had survived so far. The best answer I could give them was that I never gave up.

One evening a new resident was putting his things away in the chest of drawers besides his bed. I noticed he had an old acoustic guitar with him and asked how long he'd been playing.

"'bout as long as I could hold it." He grinned, his accent was definitely West Texas.

"Where are you from?" I asked politely.

"Midland, Texas." I was right about the accent.

After he finished stowing his gear, he sat on the edge of the bed and began to strum a few chords. I recognized the song from a lifetime ago.

When I was about five years old, my grandfather had the great pleasure of baby-sitting me one summer. It was the year my grandmother died and he was the only one available. So he took me to work with him. One day he had to be on the set of a cowboy picture at Iverson's Ranch because there was a musical number to be photographed. It was a Roy Rogers movie, back when he was the undisputed king of the cowboys.

As we arrived at the set, my Grandfather turned me over to one of the wranglers, who normally handle the horses. Without complaining that he had other things to do, the wrangler put me on the back of a Palomino pony that looked just like Roy's horse, Trigger, and told me to be very quiet. Rogers was perched on a twisted tree trunk, courtesy of the prop department, and was surrounded by his singing group "The Sons of the Pioneers" and a bewhiskered Gabby Hayes.

"Quiet on the set," the Assistant Director screamed.

When the Director called action, Roy began strumming the same chords as the man in the homeless shelter. With the Sons of the Pioneers adding a harmonious tune, he sang, "From this valley they say you are going, we will miss your bright eyes and sweet smile..."

And in the Albuquerque Opportunity Center, a place of desperation and despair, at least fifty voices picked up the song nearly sixty years later: "For they say you are taking the sunshine, that has brightened our pathway a while. Come and sit by my side if you love me. Do not hasten to bid me ado. Just remember the Red River Valley, and the cowboy who loved you so true."

Six decades in the flash of a G chord, it was though someone wrapped a blanket around the history of my life, brought it all together and wrapped it in a bow.

I knew there would be challenges ahead. I hadn't started a comeback. First I had to recover, then I needed to learn how to live with my condition, but at that moment, I knew I would somehow salvage my life and use what talent I had to make things better. It might take years, but my new arteries had lots of time left in them. I needed a plan and then I had to work it. Easier said than done, but I was on a natural high.

Later that night, one of the residents died. Nobody ever knew why.

CHAPTER THIRTY
A Month of Sundays

Three months had passed since my operation. The doctors decided I was strong enough to survive a surgery which would restore my voice. UNM Hospital wasn't taking any chances, they put their best ear, nose and throat man on the case. He'd already shoved his video camera down my throat once a month and probably knew it better than his own. Prior to the surgery the anesthesiologist gave me a little lecture.

"Now, Mr. Barrett, we're not really putting you to sleep, although the passage of time won't seem normal. You won't feel a thing and we really don't want you to do anything until it's time to test the implant. The entire surgery should take about two hours. I'll be with you all the way and it isn't as bad as it sounds."

"They're going to cut my throat," I croaked.

"Yes, but they'll sew it back up again," promised the doc.

"I suppose you want me to count backwards from 100?" I asked.

"That won't be necessary this time."

I saw him inject something into my IV and then a wave of relaxation swept over me. I remember being wheeled into the operating room and feeling some pressure on my throat, but I really couldn't understand what the surgical team was saying and my mind began to wander.

I remembered it was my first Sunday at AOC. Sunday's were always difficult, even though they gave you an extra hour to sleep. The Mission was open for breakfast, but there was nowhere to go for lunch or dinner. Sunday was a hungry day. There were rumors of a picnic for the homeless at a place called Train Park, but Billy and I couldn't find it, and according to him the rumors were never true. So we had eleven hours to pass before the bus would return us to AOC, without anything to do and nothing to eat. Between the two of us we didn't have enough money to invest in a $1 McDonald's Cheeseburger, so instead we walked through the glamorous warehouse district.

"You know, Billy, you'd think the churches would offer us something on a Sunday." I remarked as we strode past one loading dock after another.

"They don't need us to fill their pews on Sunday, they've already got a crowd."

"Don't they care if we're starving?" I asked innocently.

"Now you understand, guy, we're not on their agenda today. They'll do something nice for us tomorrow, but today we in the hands of the Lord. He will provide, so it says in the good book."

In the distance we could see a patch of green, a little pocket park.

"Why don't we go over there," I suggested, "maybe we'll find a ball to toss around."

"Ain't nothing better to do." Billy replied.

Well, there were no spare balls, but a bunch of people had started a game of slow pitch, so Billy and I sat in the bleachers and watched. It hadn't been so many years ago when I used to go to 20 or 30 games a year at Dodger

Stadium – Sandy Koufax throwing flames at nearly 100 miles an hour, Drysdale scaring the shit out of hitters, and here we were passing the day watching slow pitch. For a while it took our minds off our stomachs which, sure enough, began to grumble.

"You've never gone hungry before?" Billy said suddenly looking at me.

"No, I've been hungry, but was never unable to buy food. You know, stop at the 7-11 and pick up a snack."

"Guess it never occurred to you that some folk couldn't even do that? Not much fun is it? People on the street go hungry every day. They say we're the richest nation on Earth and yet, good human beings, supposed to be loved by the Lord, but down on their luck, go without anything to eat. Don't make much sense to me."

It got worse. A short distance from us a large African American family were having a picnic. We could smell the barbeque, hot dogs and hamburgers; the perfect lunch on a sunny Sunday afternoon.

"It's easier if you breath through your mouth." Billy told me. We both just sat there, together, but alone in our individual misery.

I put my head in my hands and tried to concentrate on the game.

"Excuse me, gentleman." It was a man from the picnic. "My family wanted to share our bounty with you."

He handed us two paper plates on which were piled the thickest hamburgers either of us had ever seen; and there were beans and potato salad. Then he handed each of us a can of Coca Cola.

I had tears in my eyes, so did Billy. "God bless you," we said simultaneously. We looked at each other.

"See, I told you, the Lord will provide," Billy said. "Bet you didn't know he was black."

"Mr. Barrett, will you please try to say the word, ah?" It was the voice of the surgeon. I didn't feel the time pass but I was flat on my back in the OR.

"Ah….ah….ah." I rumbled, my voice was as strong as James Earl Jones, you know, Darth Vader. I could talk, I wouldn't have to spend the rest of my life wheezing and croaking!

"Thank you, Mr. Barrett. Please be quiet while we finish seating the implant. You're going to be just fine."

Just fine, I thought, and now all I had to do was find a place to live. I'd be out of AOL in a month, but my life would be anything but normal.

CHAPTER THIRTY-ONE
The War Zone

My time at AOC was coming to an end. I still didn't have what I considered my normal strength, but I could get around and childhood's end was nearing. Shannon promised to find me a place, but doing so was unexpectedly hard. Everybody wanted references – well I had none in Albuquerque except the shelter and that was enough for me to get a polite no. In addition it was hard to find something under $500 a month and considering I was getting a stipend of $635 a month disability, that didn't leave much room for nights on the town. Indeed, it didn't leave much room for nights at Burger King.

My heart was sinking as we began to look in less desirable neighborhoods. I wasn't a snob, at this point, all I wanted was a modicum of safety, unfortunately all the safe neighborhoods were taken and I was left with one choice, The War Zone.

Now, before you accuse me of elitism or racism or any other kind of ism I didn't invent the name. No, that honor belongs to the Albuquerque Police Department, for The War Zone was the highest crime neighborhood in the city. The apartment we found was a hovel; three rooms, filthy, the landlady just laughed when we asked if she would clean it. I did my best, being unable to afford a cleaning service; in retrospect it could have best been cleaned with a couple of dynamite sticks.

I had no furniture at all; Shannon loaned me a 19" television set and I slept on the floor in the bedroom. Every night I was serenaded by the sound of police sirens, domestic quarrels, loud music, people fighting over drugs. In the entire time I lived there (nearly 2 1/2 years) I never went out at night with only one or two exceptions. I was plainly terrified, not a good situation for a man with a heart condition.

There were six units in the hovel and I made sure to smile at my neighbors, who looked puzzled that an Anglo was living among them. The property was littered with broken beer bottles, empty bags of potato chips, used condoms; what were the children who grew up there supposed to think?

I still had no car, and the walk to the bus stop, which was only two blocks away became a scary daily adventure. I passed mean looking tattooed men; I have nothing against tattoos but these were representing some of the most vicious gangs in Albuquerque. One of them "19" was made up of former Columbians who took great pleasure in torturing their victims before killing them. I never made eye contact, and I can assume the only reason I survived was became I looked harmless – although I'm sure these guys would have killed me anyways, if that had been their mood.

On Sundays they would parade with their girl friends and the kids they had together. While I'm no sociologist, I feel certain that the coming generations are going to suffer for all the children born out of wedlock, who never had a real childhood. I had some pleasant memories at least, what were their's?

There were plenty of homeless in the area, who probably knew they were taking their lives in their hands, if they stayed in the area after dark. Murders, rapes, muggings were common, some worse than others. Drugs were everywhere. I remember one afternoon walking back from the bus stop and seeing at least four different groups smoking from a crack pipe. All I wanted to do was to get home, lock the door and put a chair I'd acquired in front of it. I had no weapon and kept thinking about purchasing a gun, but on my meager allowance couldn't afford it.

At least at the shelter I had people to talk to, but here I became a hermit. I stayed in, read a lot of books, and listened to the sounds of mayhem just outside my window. The library, which was my only source of entertainment was two blocks away, and believe me I walked as fast as I could and only during the day. Along the way I passed neat little houses, well kept, but with bars on the windows and signs warning of vicious dogs on the gates. The owners were as terrified as I, but at least they had cable television to keep them occupied.

I was still experiencing a lot of fatigue. By three in the afternoon, I was usually exhausted. I knew I couldn't keep going like this, eventually I had to find work, still I didn't know what I could do or even if I had the physical strength to do it.

Gradually, Shannon and Bren had become like family to me. They would take me out for breakfast, knowing I couldn't afford it myself. I have never met two more genuinely generous people with bigger hearts. I think it had gone beyond the point where they felt sorry for me. We all got along so well that our relationship was truly familial, although in a way I had never known. The main problem was that Bren lived in Rio Rancho with her boyfriend Jim, a terrific guy, who would become a physicians assistant. Although it was only 20 miles away, for me it might as well have been on Pluto.

That first month in the war zone was the loneliest time I can remember. I didn't speak to anybody and they didn't speak to me. I was truly a curiosity, an Anglo living in the Barrio. The first really pleasurable day was Thanksgiving.

Shannon was kind enough to drive me to her mother's and there we had a traditional Thanksgiving dinner. It was a small party, Cousins Karen, Al and Gordon, two nice guys who treated me as though I belonged. We talked and ate; everyone did their best to make me feel a part of something. I still had an ounce of humanity left after everything that had happened and it was nice to exercise it. There was still an uncertain future, but on this occasion, as opposed to my Thanksgiving celebrations of the past, I felt I really had something for which to give thanks. I was alive, against all odds, and I had a small opportunity to make my way back. I knew it wouldn't be easy but I wanted to get back into television and then do something meaningful. My road was paved with good intentions, but yes, there was still some hell ahead.

CHAPTER THIRTY-TWO
Redemption's Beginning

After more than a month living in a run down slum of an apartment, in the most dangerous neighborhood in Albuquerque, I decided that recovering or not I needed a job. I was getting $635 a month disability plus $90 a month in food stamps. I had no car, but by now was an expert on the bus system. Prior to my heart attack I didn't look my age, but now I certainly did and getting a senior's pass for the bus proved no problem. I started looking at retail jobs for which I had an affinity. What I didn't want was a position that required heavy lifting because in my current condition I simply couldn't do it, nor did I want to end up selling shoes – to me that was the worst job I could think of.

One day in October I spotted an ad for Comp USA, a store that sold electronics (computers, printers and televisions). Televisions! I knew something about them and called to set up an interview.

It took two buses to get to the store. I had to start out on the Central Avenue bus, not the most mellow of experiences. It was on that bus that I saw a fight break out between a very stupid white man and four big African Americans. He was yelling racial epithets at their girlfriends and that didn't last very long. What did he expect? Three of them picked him up and physically threw him off the bus, while it was moving. Every one else stayed quiet, since we didn't want to incur anyone's attention ourselves.

At last, I switched to the San Mateo bus and took a seat behind the driver, which I figured was the safest place to be. Without incident we pushed up San Mateo Boulevard and came to my stop, just below Menaul. To the left was a huge outdoor mall with dozens of different stores. A quarter of a mile down was a giant store with the logo of Comp USA.

I'm seldom nervous before an interview, but this time I was. If it was just going to be another of those "you're overqualified for this job" that was going to be a defeat. I knew it was coming, but I had to find a way to deflect it. So as I walked past one retail store after another, my mind was racing to come with an answer.

"Come on Barrett," I said to myself, "you've pitched the presidents of studios and networks. This guy needs help and you know you'll do the job no matter what it is. Your ego has been long crushed by the events of the past seven months. You're not a superstar, but your not a schlub either.

Arriving on time I met a man in his thirties, good looking, who shaved what little hair he had left into a Yul Brynner. He reached out and gave me a firm handshake. There was something about this guy that I really liked, but first I had to get him to like me. As is my style in meetings I assume a very relaxed atmosphere – to put him at ease.

Charles Petit III leaned back in his chair. "Tell me about yourself Don. Where did you go to school?"

"Well Charles I did my undergraduate work at California State University at Northridge and then I got a scholarship to the Royal College of Music in London. I spent two years there and then went touring with various orchestras."

"What happened, how come you aren't conducting the Albuquerque Symphony?" He asked without expression.

"When I came back to the United States there was no real demand for American born conductors. Leonard Bernstein was the only high profile guy with an American Pedigree. So after knocking my heads against enough hiring committees, I decided to take a job at Pyramid Films. Pyramid produced mostly educational product, but they began to branch out. I was involved in making 'Scared Straight' which went on to become one of two shows to win both an 'Academy Award' and an 'Emmy Award'. The other two-time winner was carried by Pyramid too."

I think he was enjoying my story or possibly he thought he was in the presence of one of the world's great bullshit artists. I had to convince him of my sincerity.

"You left Pyramid Films at some point, correct?"

"Yes, because of my family's history in entertainment I wangled a job at Dick Clark Productions. I was a lowly researcher at first, but I worked my way up. Dick and I had a mutual interest in old television and he was building an archive of an impressive size. Part of my time I spend administrating the archive, putting in a film to tape transfer and editing system, and cataloging the shows. It meant I got to relive my childhood, watching every rock 'n' roll star from Bill Halley and the Comets, to a rare performance by Buddy Holly and of course, the wild man, Jerry Lee Lewis. Ultimately I was given the honor of producing the annual Christmas Show. Suddenly I was the boss and all the people with whom I worked were there to support me.

"The show was full of surprises. We got the President of NBC, Brandon Tartikoff to put in a cameo appearance, and we got Michael Jackson to clear his hit, 'Santa Claus is Coming to Town' for the end credits. This was possible because my Uncle, years ago, had written a song for Michael that went to #1 and stayed there for months. It was a song about a boy and a rat, and was simply called 'Ben'. Anyway, the day after the Christmas Show I found my office empty. I was confused; I thought I'd been fired, but there was a note on the wall to go downstairs and see my boss.

I went into his office and low and behold he and our Executive Producer, were waiting for me. Gulp. They took me by the hand and led to a sumptuous office on producer's row. I had arrived.

"That's quite a story, I don't hear many like that when I'm interviewing." Charles said.

"After Clark, I went to work for Johnny Carson for a short time and then did a lot of independent features for the home video market. About seven months ago I got murdered in a divorce and here I am, ready to bring the same passion for performance to COMP USA."

"You sold me, Don. When can you start?" Charles asked, a big smile on his face.

"What time is it?" I asked.

CHAPTER THIRTY-THREE
COMP USA

In this managerial wisdom, Charles decided I should take over television sales. At first it was a little grueling for me, standing on my feet all day simply whacked me out. Most of the other employees ranged from early 20's to 30's and I knew I couldn't keep up with them, unless I used my knowledge of the product to sell and a little diplomacy to help with the heavy lifting. I had always lived with the conceit that I could talk to anyone, now it would be put to the test.

At the time I took up my post our TV sales were pathetic. Comparably priced, no one knew how to sell them. Instead of a minimum of one TV a day, we're selling at a rate of two TV's a month. One of the big problems was they were playing movies through the televisions that didn't catch the eye. In fact, the young associates, were playing movies they wanted to see. I drew their ire by purchasing a blue ray disk of Star Wars III with my own money. We had plenty of Blue Ray players in the store and I hooked one up. Immediately customers from 5-70 were parking themselves in front of the sets. They had never seen such quality in a television picture and were amazed. I took a lot of flack for doing it, but Charles stood behind me all the way. The bottom line was TV Sales were now up to two a day, a massive improvement.

In addition, I could bring special knowledge to the buyers, who couldn't decide between one brand and another. Some stores actually detune certain brands they don't want to sell and up tune others they do, usually on the basis

149

of where they make the most profit. Again with Charles watching my back, I came in one morning and did a thorough set up so each TV was giving us its best.

More than once customers asked me about that.

"Because some TV sellers only max out the set on the models they want to sell. Those look better and you buy them. At COMP USA we want you to make a decision based upon a fair comparison. No tricks."

I can't tell you how much the customers appreciated that. Some came back for second and third sets.

"Tell your friends, our prices are honest and so are our displays."

Well, it must have worked, because sales of televisions kept going up and up.

Then one day, Charles called me into his office, and said.

"I can't tell you how pleased we are about the way you're selling TV's and it's come to the attention of COMP USA management. We've gone from number 34 in sales in our region to number 4. They want to fly you to Dallas for a seminar on television and perhaps tell you that you're on a management track."

Wow, I was surprised and elated. I thought it would take much longer to get anyone's attention. At the seminar something else happened, which was very unexpected. At the beginning we were all asked about our background. I stood and simply said, "I've done film, network television, and home video as a writer, producer and director, oh and my favorite interest is astronomy."

The man throwing the seminar was quite impressed and from there on, every time he made a statement, he would look to me for verification. I did help him out once or twice on subjects like the vertical synch interval, or the meaning of IRE units. When the seminar was over and we were getting together our ditty bags, the Regional Vice President of the company came over and whispered into my ear, "How'd you like to live in Dallas?"

I replied, "I'd be honored." It was November of 2007 and I was flying high as a kite. First we'd have to wait for the Christmas season to pass, then a management training course, but I believed I was on track to middle management in a national company. I don't know if I arrived home before the jet put down at the Albuquerque Sunport, but it is entirely possible. Considering the events of the last seven months this was northing short of a miracle.

I had made a pact with myself to work my ass off during the holiday season. The television section had gone from one every two weeks to three and four per day. Every time I would tote one up to the cash register for sale, I would look directly into Charles Office, and he would just smile and shake his head.

I felt good, I felt productive and with all the people I was meeting, I was a part of Albuquerque.

It was my birthday, Shannon and her mother were taking me out to dinner. There were lots of reasons to celebrate. I had a job, I was making money, I had bought an old jalopy of a car (no more waiting for the bus in 8 degree weather). Most importantly, I thought I had found a way up, out of the sales floor into management, even if I had to move to Dallas. Hell I could become a Cowboy fan, the Rams weren't much to talk about anyway, mired in last place.

After Dinner we stopped back at COMP USA, so I could pick up some material. Everybody's head was down, I didn't see a single smile.

What's going on, I asked one of the managers. She drew a deep sigh, the kind one does when really bad news is to be passed on.

"You ever heard of Carlos Slim?" He asked.

"Can't say that I have."

"Well, he's a Mexican billionaire and he owns us. The other day he decided he wanted out of the business, so we're closing."

"What!" I was astonished. "This is a valuable property. Why doesn't he just sell us."

"Shit, I don't know. The liquidators will be in first of the year. They're throwing us all onto the streets."

So my hopes of making it into middle management were just that hopes. By the time I was ready, middle management and the company will have disappeared. I had done so well. I sold out the entire warehouse inventory of HDTV's, and now my reward was having no place to go. One more rock in the road; a little bit of hell.

CHAPTER THIRTY-FOUR
Carole for Another Christmas

Yes, the "e" in Carole is intentional, an homage to my first girlfriend. I was so in love, I drove from San Francisco to Los Angeles in my Triumph Spitfire through a pounding rain just so I could knock on her window at 3:00 in the morning. This was two years before Dustin Hoffman did almost the same thing in "The Graduate," but I'm not claiming a steal.

Anyway, the yuletide was upon us. I always loved Christmas, which may seem funny for a Jew, but like a lot of Hollywood Jews we celebrated a secular version of the Christmas. Besides there were plenty of non-Jews in my family. My Aunt Betty was the best cook and she was Lutheran, and for goodness sake my Uncle Ronnie was Jamaican – none of that mattered to me. I loved the music, the traditions, the tree and especially the presents. Throughout my childhood, every Christmas was celebrated at Uncle Walter's mansion, with a fifteen foot tree and literally hundreds of presents underneath. The whole family would show and everyone would dress for the occasion.

I used to have a recurring dream that all the presents were handed out and I received nothing. That actually happened one year, but I won't dwell on that.

Christmas 2007 was rather different. For one thing I'd been bombarded with carols at the store, but they were the same ones over and over and none of them were my favorites. Bing Crosby crooned "White Christmas" endlessly, Burl Ives sang "Here Comes Santa Claus" a hundred times (the song actually belonged to Gene Autry – a family friend who gave my Grandfather season tickets when he bought the old Los Angeles Angels). No my favorites were always, "Oh Holy Night," the old English folk favorite "On Christmas Night All Christians Sing to Hear the News the Angels Bring" and "Oh Tannenbaum." They never played those at Comp USA and that was disappointing.

Black Friday brought out the worst in people. They elbowed each other to get to the specials and then got very pissed off when the object of their desire was sold out. Not being Christian I shouldn't comment, but I'm sure that's not what the holiday is supposed to be about. Fortunately, once the big rush was over it got more mellow and people gradually assumed the Christmas spirit. A lot of Merry Christmases were exchanged, and people seemed to smile a lot more. Selling televisions was a joy because I knew how much pleasure those big flat screens would bring their owners.

One thing that got my attention was the way people peered from television to television trying to decide which had the best picture. Now I've been looking at critical monitors all my life and once they are tweaked, it's nearly impossible to tell the difference. The reason televisions don't look the same in the store is they haven't been properly adjusted. The problem was: these TV's were adjusted and the differences were tiny. Still people were going nuts trying to see the which was better the Sony or the Mitsubishi. They'd ask me which looked better to me and I'd always answer: "The only thing that counts is what looks better to you."

Finally, it was Christmas and again Shannon took me out to her mothers. There was the same small contingent, although some of Jim's family showed up. I wonder if they could figure out who I was and what I was doing there. I think I was experiencing the holiday like no other. In the past year I had lost everything, my home, my family, my money and my health and here I was, alive to celebrate another Christmas. I had a job, at least for a while, and soon I'd be able to buy a better car, as I had been saving what little I earned. It was truly a time of rejoicing for me; my life had been like trying to cross the Hollywood Freeway at rush hour and somehow, someway I think I made it.

So when the turkey was brought out I savored it like never before. Food tasted better. There was, at last, some hope in my life, but that voice continued inside my head:

"It isn't over until it's over."

But would it ever be over? What could I attain that would finally grant me peace? It wasn't going to be enough just to be making television shows again. I needed something more to justify the suffering and the lessons I had learned. I had begun to change, or to use a word that Leonard Bernstein was fond of: transmogrify. Where that change would lead me I didn't know, but I was vaguely aware of something important. I was no longer the shallow "Hollywood type," lacking in real world knowledge or empathy. I no longer needed to be seen around the beautiful, celebrated and worshiped. Maybe, just maybe I was becoming a better person – or was that too much to hope for?

CHAPTER THIRTY-FIVE
Liquidation

The news had come like a shockwave across a clear pool. Happy Birthday Donald. The store would have four months to liquidate and close its doors forever. Of course the main question on everybody's lips was "Why?" The answer was actually simple. The chain was owned by Carlos Slim, a Mexican billionaire who simply got tired of being in the electronics business. A swish of his pen and thousands of people would be out of work.

I had made friends there, not the least of which was a fellow named Matt. He was young, married and very smart. Things being as they were he and his wife might have been thinking about children. Now they were facing an unknown future. It occurred to me more than once, that they could wind up on the street, but hopefully their families could keep them afloat for a little while.

Liquidating a store can actually be fun, if you don't dwell on the fact that with each day the end is coming closer and closer. The more the prices drop the easier it is to sell, but then there are those customers who want to wait until the last nanosecond, before they'll commit to a purchase. Finally, when they are ready the item is gone. More often than not they are pissed and can't wait to take it out on somebody – like me.

"I told you to keep an eye on the Mitsubishi 55" HDTV, didn't I"

"Sorry sir it sold on my day off."

"Well you should have told everyone in the store; I tell you the people who work here are dumb as mules."

That's the first time in my life anybody had called me dumb. I wanted to grab this guy by the collar and offer to give him $1000 for every IQ point, he was higher than me and to take $1000 for each point I was higher than him; nah I'd have been fired and he would have lost his shirt, still it was tempting.

Then love blossomed, if for only a moment. Love was the last thing on my mind since my marriage went TNT, but there she was. A beautiful intelligent redhead (redheads have always been my downfall, I married one, I must have gone out with ten others – I never knew why, but they sure had an attraction). She owned her own consulting firm and wanted to buy two televisions. I steered her towards the best ones we had on the floor, while holding a fascinating conversation on our favorite islands in the South Pacific. She was beautiful, classy and there was a spark.

So when the bill came to nearly $10,000 she didn't bat an eye lid, rather she pulled out an American Express Platinum and whooshed it through the card reader, and I helped her load a brand new Range Rover. My heart was fluttering – dare I ask this gorgeous woman out. In the days, pre-Jackie, I would have in a heart beat, but in the intervening years my ego had taken such a brutalizing, that it wasn't a done deal. Thank God for aggressive women. She gave me her card and a warm hug and said we should get together sometime.

The next day she called, but it wasn't the sweet voice I expected to hear; it was the voice of the dragon.

"One of the sets you've sold me doesn't work, it doesn't turn on."

"Give me a minute with my manager to make this right."

I went over to Charles and told him the story. "It's up to the liquidator." He responded.

"Charles, we wouldn't drop a piece of broken merchandise on a customer that just spent ten large?"

Charles sighed, "It's not up to me anymore. Talk to the liquidator."

I spoke with the man, an otherwise nice fellow, who didn't seem too concerned. "She'll have to take it to the factory. There's a factory representative in town.

I called her back with the good news, which she seemed to be taking rather well, I told her if it were up to me she could return the set for a refund, but I was just another pawn of Carlos Slim. I offered to go to Mexico and kick his ass. After all, she was out $5,000.

The factory rep said the TV was dead from the time it was assembled so he couldn't help. Perhaps she'd like to check with the manufacturer. The poor lady was getting what the French call ze runaround.

I called her back and told her what was going on and expressed my greatest apologies. She wasn't having any, and my romance sprouted wings and flew away.

So my first chance at some sort of interpersonal normalcy was gone with the last winds of winter. Now I would have to throw myself into the thankless job of emptying a warehouse, and then going on the hunt for new work in a down economy that was getting worse.

I set a store record selling seven televisions in one day, but there were no trophies, no congratulations. For the rest of the staff I was taking them one day closer to disappointment.

There was one guy, whom I liked him very much. He was scarcely 20 years old and his girlfriend was about to have a baby. He didn't know whether to stay or run.

"Do you love her?" I asked him one day in the break room.

"Oh yes, I'm just not ready to be a father."

"Believe me nobody is just ready. Do you think I was ready when I was twice your age?"

"So Don, what did you do?"

"I was a fucking man about it. I stayed with her through 22 hours of labor and when the time came, I cut the chord."

"Didn't that make you sick?" He asked.

"It's nature, my friend, and I owed it to my wife and daughter. No matter what has happened since, that was the proudest moment of my life. You'll see. Forget what the feminists tell you, there are differences between men and women. Now it's your time to be a man and be there for your woman and child. If Gloria Steinem doesn't like it, well fuck her."

He started to laugh, he'd never heard me swear before. He laughed and laughed and collapsed into the chair. Two days later he came up to me in the break room and planted a big kiss on my cheek.

"Thanks." He said.

"For what?" I asked.

"For teaching me to be man."

"You always had it in you Pal – you just had to find it."

"We're naming the baby Austin, 'cause that's the name you liked.

The last month of liquidation was a virtual zoo. One product after another went out of stock, much to the annoyance of the customers who expected us to hold everything for them. The retail public is, for the most part, very unforgiving. They want what they want and they've been conditioned to get it. In the meantime, all of us were concerned about what we'd be doing next.

Charles actually set up some interviews and I successfully landed a job, although at the time I didn't know it would be the job from hell. One day after the store closed, and was being cleaned for the next owner, we were sitting around telling stories. When my turn came, I decided, just for fun to reveal something they didn't know about me or I would have been pestered the entire time I was there. It was the first time since coming to Albuquerque, that I really let on anything substantive about the life I used to lead.

"Okay, I have an unusual story about how I was born. I came from a show business family that worked in film, television and yes, radio, when it was the equivalent of television without pictures.

"My mother was nine months pregnant and my uncle was watching over her since my father was out of town. Uncle Walter was the musical director of the Phil Harris-Alice Faye Show which was a big hit comedy on Sunday nights. It was Friday and they were doing the dress rehearsal, the last one before the show.

"Right in the middle of everything my mother goes into labor. Phil Harris, the star of the show, stops the proceedings, which is rather unheard of, and he, my uncle, and that week's guest star rushed my mother to the hospital. While she was being wheeled into the delivery room, these wild and crazy guys stole three sets of surgeon's greens and actually went in to watch the birth. This was long before father's were permitted anywhere near a delivery room. In those ancient times they had to sit in the waiting room smoking cigarettes.

"It was a normal birth with the three "wise guys" standing around looking on. From what my mother told me, the first human face I ever saw was the guest star on that week's show – Jack Benny."

The one's who were old enough to remember Benny laughed and laughed. The others just looked quizzically. I couldn't help but reflect how far I had come from those magical days of childhood and still I wondered how I would ever get them back.

CHAPTER THIRTY-SIX
My Love – The Internet

I'll admit it, love has been an unending quest, one that has consumed my entire life. Other than my mother and grandfather, I can't think of anybody who really loved me as a child. Certainly my father didn't. I was an inconvenience he managed to avoid by plunking himself down on the East Coast, and placing a continent between us. Although I wrote him many letters, I can't think of more than a handful I ever received. I realize this is not such an unusual situation in the 21st century, but in the time of my childhood, it was not the way things were. The day I graduated elementary school, I was the only child not to have a father in attendance and believe me, I knew it.

Going back as far as my high school days, I was never a particularly popular kid. I'm sure I had something of an inferiority complex generated by the lack of a support system and a happy family. Oh I went out every once in a while, but nothing much to speak about. I did have one or two relationships that you could call boyfriend-girlfriend but it didn't last. I didn't start dating in a big way until I started working at my chosen profession. To this day, I feel quite sure that much of what passed for my attraction was what I did and the people I knew.

Although we've all been exposed to the movies and its pantheon of gods and goddesses, most of us don't look like those people, unless of course you live in Los Angeles and everyone expects you to. I was okay, but I never wanted to be in front of the camera and although I was in a couple of extremely forgettable movies ("The Thrill Killers" and "The Incredibly

161

Strange Creatures that Gave Up Living and Became Mixed Up Zombies" – honest that was the title), I knew I belonged behind the scenes.

Yet, through my 20's and 30's I dated lots of beautiful women and traveled with them all over the world, so what do I have to complain about? When I met Jackie, I thought I'd hit the jackpot. She was beautiful and bright, and maybe if we'd have been more alike, we'd still be together. I am always envious of anyone who has enjoyed a long happy marriage.

Now, after the many traumatic shocks I endured, my interest in the opposite sex was once again abloom, but I was more than twenty years out of practice in dating. How could I meet women who might want to go out with me. With all the scars on my arms and legs from my surgeries I was certainly no spring chicken, indeed I thought of myself as more of a winter carcass. Still I was certain there were women somewhere that would find me attractive or at least interesting.

There were a few problems. Though now I had a little money I was not about to attack the dating scene with the avidity of my youth. Although I had upgraded from my first Albuquerque car I was driving a heap, a clunker that wouldn't attract a gopher. Finally, I wasn't working in a glamorous profession and couldn't exactly invite a date to the Academy Awards. So I turned to the internet, knowing nothing.

First rule of internet dating: everybody lies, either about their height, weight, number of marriages, number of teeth and forget about the picture they put on their profile. One even had the audacity to place a rather famous shot of Marilyn Monroe. I sent her an email and asked her why. She actually replied – I didn't expect one – and said that her girlfriend said she looked like Marilyn. So, I replied, "Why don't you put up a picture of yourself?"

Her answer: "I get more emails this way."

After a few more foiled attempts at landing a date, I finally arranged to meet a woman for coffee at a nearby Starbucks. We had a fine conversation and I was beginning to think that there might be something to this internet dating.

Then out of nowhere she says, "I can't possibly get in a relationship with you."

"Oh," I asked, "Wherefore not?"

"Your height. You're an inch shorter than me and that makes you ineligible." She was beautiful and very tall.

"I had no idea it was such an issue."

"Oh yes, Don, you're the perfect package. You're just too short."

Well, so much for logic. My next few dates didn't turn out much better. One was a vegan, so I could never have stayed with her on the diet. Another was a Wiccan and only wanted to talk about the spirituality of wood, a subject good for maybe five minutes but two hours?

I was fighting a lost cause. Remember I was driving a broken down car that I'm sure no self-respecting woman would want to be seen in. Maybe, I should try dating out of town, that way my car wouldn't be an issue.

So after much flirting over the internet I finally got a date with a woman who lived in Phoenix. The email interchange got hot and heavy and I thought finally there would be some dalliance in my life. So I practically bankrupted myself with new clothes not to mention the airfare to Phoenix and a nice hotel (four stars!).

I should have known something was up when she failed to meet me at the airport, forcing me to spend another $40 on a taxi ride to Camelback. Finally, I get a call at the hotel and she promised to be over in an hour. I wait, an hour goes by, then two. I try unsuccessfully to call her.

Then there's a knock on my door. I open it, and there she is. Very attractive, well worth the wait.

She stares longingly into my eyes and says, "You're not my type," and closes the door. End of date.

It wasn't all bad though. I had the great pleasure of meeting a woman with whom I shared a close friendship for more than a year. She was quite wealthy and it showed in her home. A beautiful custom built house it abutted the Cibola National Forest, so nothing would ever destroy her view.

And what a view it was. Although not everybody would find great beauty in pinion and sage, it was arrayed against the most beautiful part of the southern Rockies. At night we would sit on a lounge chair outside and I would give her a tour of the sky. This was something I'd been doing for people since the age of ten, when I was presented with a telescope for my birthday.

The stars are extremely important to me. If the truth be told, the real reason I lived in Malibu all those years ago wasn't to have celebrity neighbors or movie stars on the block, but because the sky was dark, away from the blinding city lights of Los Angeles. In the summer, the Milky Way, that sparkling band of countless stars that make up our galaxy, would appear to arch across the sky only to be swallowed by the great Pacific. Almost as soon as we moved in, I bought a ten inch telescope and taught Jackie and later Torrey how to use it. One of my fondest memories of Malibu was taking a very young Torrey out into the back yard with the stars blazing overhead. Stealing a line from "Roots" I said, "Behold Torrey Barrett, the only thing greater than thou."

Getting back to my lady friend, I learned so much from her. She was a great story teller, who had gone to school in Leningrad (now St. Petersburg) during the height of the Cold War. She even had a run-in with the KGB. Her perspective on those times, it being what the government wanted her to know, was so different than mine.

Perhaps the most wonderful thing about her was her closeness to nature. She would put out bird seed every day and then could name every variety of bird that appeared. Once I showed her a video I'd shot in Africa along the Serengeti Plain and she knew the name of every animal. More importantly she had a manner which made me feel peaceful inside. That our friendship ended was a personal tragedy, and the way it ended only compounded my feeling that inside of every human being is a little insanity.

She was going to a business convention and asked me if I wanted to house-sit. Of course I said yes, it was like staying at the Ahwahnee or the Old Faithful Inn. During the day there were no sounds of traffic, only birdsong and the thrumming of wings. At night the stars painted a breathtaking portrait over the dome of the sky.

One night I went outside for a moment of stargazing before going to bed. I closed the sliding door behind me so as not to let out the cat. Somehow the door latch locked and I was locked out on the patio with no way back in. It was getting cold with an expected low of about 20F. I was wearing a "T" Shirt and a pair of jeans with no shoes. I tried everything I could think of to get back in the house, but it had become a matter of life and death.

I'd invited a friend named Liz to see the house and check out the stars with me. She was also lightly dressed and the fact is neither of us would have survived the night. I owed it to her and myself to get back in the house by any means necessary. I found a brick and after about three swings at a small double paned window broke through. Fortunately, Liz was small enough to get inside and open the door.

The incident precipitated the end of that friendship since I had violated the spirit of the house. I miss the woman to this day, but I know I'll never be invited back and that is a sadness with which I will have to live.

As for my friend Liz, she thought it was a gross over-reaction, but you never what people will do in a given situation. That was the end of my internet dating. Being just a tad too old to hang out in bars, I became very lonely, a condition which has not changed as I write these words. As for Liz, she's a magic coral island. A world within a circle, one that I will never really know.

CHAPTER THIRTY-SEVEN
Medium on the Telephone

I've always hated the telephone. Oh yes, I can talk as well as anyone, but I can't see the face or the body language, so I never really know how the person is reacting except by the tone of their voice. Having said that, the job Charles arranged for me to get was working in the Albuquerque call center for Comcast.

Before this job I had never thought much about Comcast. It's a vertically integrated communications company that has 33 million cable subscribers, but has also something like ten cable networks. Indeed, as of this writing, they are working their way through the Securities and Exchange Commission to purchase a controlling interest in NBC Universal, which means that it will be the King Kong of Television. My hope was that by doing a decent job in the call center I could worm my way into the production end. I figured it wouldn't be so bad having a high paying job working for King Kong as long as he didn't want to take me to the top of the Empire State Building without an elevator.

Believe me, I had no concept of what a call center was like. I assumed people called in, politely paid their bills, purchased extra features for their cable, ordered movies and went about their day. Fifty percent of the time that's exactly what they did, the other fifty percent I was an unwilling participant in a drama that belonged on an "X" rated television show, and since I was the voice that represented the company, all the vile, vitriol and hatred they had for the company was expended on me.

After a month's worth of training for 200 possible call-in scenarios, I was finally put on the phones. For the first time in my life I was actually nervous talking to somebody. Thank goodness the first call was only a lady wishing to pay her bill. That I could handle. A few calls later the drama was ramped up.

"I paid for movies on demand and now I'm demanding a movie, which the damn screen says I can't have. Who the fuck do you think you are preventing me from seeing my movie and what are you going to do about it."

"Well, sir, let me look on my computer and see if there's a problem."

"Of course there's a problem. I can't see the fucking movie."

"Yes sir, just a moment."

A check of the computer screen showed the customer was 90 days past due and his "on demand" service had been suspended.

"Excuse me, sir, but you have a bill that's over 90 days. Your service has been suspended until you pay it. I can take a payment from you now and you'll be able to see your movie."

"You can take a payment! Well fuck you!" (Clunk)

Right then and there I knew I hated the job. I wasn't used to taking that kind of abuse from a total stranger. The only good I could find in the situation was that this guy wasn't going to see his movie anytime soon.

I did my best to make friends at Comcast, but it was difficult. The phone would sit there silent, and you'd never know when it would ring, what thoughts it would interrupt. You were a slave to an inanimate object and what kind of person would be on the other end of the line was the ultimate crap shoot. Sometimes they were angry, sometimes in tears, and every once in a while I had to play psychologist for someone who was stepping too close to the abyss.

One call came in that nearly put me in tears. A lady with a pleasant southern accent wanted to know the extent of her bill.

"Let me see, ma'am for November your bill was $319.95"

"What! That's impossible! How could it be over three hundred dollars?"

"Well your basic bill is $59.95 with tax it comes to $63.40, but there are dozens of adult movies on demand at $10 each."

"That's impossible, I live with my eight year old son, and he's too young to know about those things." She implored.

"Hmmm, do you work at night by any chance, ma'am." I asked evenly.

"Why yes I do."

"Does someone sit with your son?"

"My boyfriend," she replied as a light bulb went off in her head.

"Have you blocked those adult channels with a pin code?" I needed to know.

"No, I didn't think I needed to. Just a moment…"

I could hear some shouts in the background, most of it muffled, but clearly she was asking her boyfriend if he was watching porn on her nickel. She came back on the line.

"I don't know how to say this, but he's been watching those movies with my eight year old son. Oh good Lord, what am I doing to do?"

At that moment I ceased being an employee of Comcast and tried to defuse the situation; more importantly I wanted to help this woman who was a stranger to me (the old me of Malibu and Las Vegas would have demanded the money and stayed on script).

"Look, ma'am, I can try and get you a one time credit since you didn't know that you're bill was being run up, but on a personal note, you need to think long and hard about this man and whether he's harming your son. It's none of my business, but you should also get your boy some counseling. This isn't good for him and could affect the rest of his life."

"Thank you, sir, I'll do that. What is your name?"

"My first name is Don, I'm not permitted to give out my last name."

"Jesus bless you Don." She hung up the phone. How could anyone do that to a young boy. I was shaken. I had to leave my station. I went to my supervisor to get her bill adjusted and related the story.

"I've heard it all before," she said. "We'll issue the credit but if it happens again, her account is history."

"Again? Don't you think she'll throw him out?"

"Don, for an older fellow you are naive. I'll bet the same thing happens next month."

She was right; it did.

Possibly the most unusual call I took at Comcast was on a Saturday night. There was an Ultimate Fighting Championship on pay per view costing $44.95 and we literally couldn't keep up with the demand for viewers. For hours every call was about the UFC and would I please send the signal to the cable box so someone could see it. People were having parties – blood parties as these fights were as raw as gladiators in the arena. The only difference was they weren't to the death.

Once the telecast started the calls dropped off, except for the panic calls from people whose cable boxes had malfunctioned. We did what could to "hit" the box with a reset signal, but that only worked part of the time. Otherwise a technician would have to be sent and that could take days. Of course, the customer would get a credit, but that didn't help in one particular case.

"Hey man, I've got fifty people here to see the fight and it don't work."

"Let me try sending a signal to your cable box and see if it doesn't solve the problem."

"No, it still don't work."

I tried again and again, every trick in the book and nothing worked. I finally had to tell the customer that we'd send out a technician on Tuesday afternoon.

"You don't understand, man, I charged these fifty people $25 each to come see the fight and party."

"Well sir, all I can suggest is that you refund their money." I replied not knowing what else to say.

"No man, you see I spent the money, now these guys are gonna kick my ass, maybe kill me. What am I gonna do?" He pleaded.

Whoa, fifty men with their androgens and adrenalin flowing, each of whom had been taken for $25, that was serious – and it wasn't the guy's fault. It was ours.

"Call 911 and run like hell," was the only advice left in my arsenal.

The next day I read in the paper about a man who'd been beaten to death. I hoped against hope it wasn't the guy I'd spoken too. I had presents to buy for my new family, and didn't want the ghost of customers' past hanging over me.

By October it was apparent that the phone center and I were not a marriage made in heaven. I got tired of the repetitious calls and most especially of the abusive ones. Now I know that every call center for every product gets its share of abusive calls, but I seriously wonder whether management ever gives a thought to what that does to the operators. Being sworn at in the worst possible way raises blood pressure and not being able to swear back makes it only worse. Wouldn't it be better that when a customer crosses the line, the operator would be able to tell them that that had become abusive and the call was being terminated. Wow, I can hear every phone operator in the country cheering.

The bottom line is that I was lousy on the phones. It wasn't a job for which I was suited and day after day I was getting called in by my supervisor to be encouraged to sell more telephones to people who were so pissed off about their service that they would have simply hung up or cursed me out. I explained that when I applied for the job, I'd been told that after six months I could transfer to television production. Well, when my six months arrived, I had so many demerits for phones I hadn't sold that I would now have to wait another year. The job was giving me heart palpitations, and heaven knows that's something I didn't need. I resigned in lieu of getting fired; a first in my entire life. Today, when I talk to someone at a call center I am as courteous and nice as I can be. I discovered what motivated me to help a customer above and beyond and it's no great secret. Simple humanity. They're going to get 100+ calls a day and 50% are going to irritate them. I want to be the call that stands out as nice and incidentally gets something accomplished. So I left the call center realizing I wasn't going to make as good money anywhere else except in my chosen profession – the question was how to get back in the groove. Christmas was coming, the low season for television production. Maybe if I grew a white beard I could pass as Santa Claus.

CHAPTER THIRTY-EIGHT
Would You do it for a J.C. Penney?

Christmas was coming once again and I knew stores would be hiring extra help. I dreaded going through another of those horrible Christmas rushes. I was still living in the war zone and was lonely enough that I was willing to continue going out with internet women, but I would need a decent car in which to squire them around.

The Great American Retailer, J.C. Penney was hiring for the season and although I knew the work would push me to the edges of whatever fatigue I could withstand, I applied anyway. At the time I thought I was fortunate, since they placed me in their local home wares store, what I didn't realize was how little I know about home wares. Hell, with all my education and supposed sophistication I didn't know what a duvet was! Recalling the ancient words of my deceased uncle, "I had a lot to learn."

The management was somewhat patient, although this was their busiest time of year. I'd been through the Christmas season at Comp USA and thought I could handle it, but I came to realize that my old job was part of the suburbs of the great retail empires. I was now to be thrown right into the combat zone without basic training or even a clue of what would be involved.

I've heard it said that "Black Friday" was so named because it was the day that retailers profitability went from the red to the black. I didn't believe it then and I don't believe it now. Black Friday brings out the worst in otherwise

172

sane people. There's a old saying in the stock market, "Don't buy at the very bottom or sell at the very top." What it means, of course, is that either end of the scale in unpredictable. That wisdom was lost on those who lined up at 3:00 AM in freezing weather, the day after stuffing down that Thanksgiving turkey with all the fixings.

As for me, it is the last day I would ever consider shopping, but then I hate crowds, especially aggressive ones. I could just see myself having a heart attack and being stepped over by someone who wanted the world's best deal on a toaster oven, but this particular Black Friday I had no choice. I was to be at the store at 2:30 AM, prepared for the single most chaotic day of the retail year.

I'd heard stories: last year a woman was trampled to death at a Wal-Mart in New Jersey, but that was Newark, Albuquerque was supposed to be more laid back. It wasn't. Arriving at the store, I noticed the line snaked around the parking lot and back. It was so cold, I was wearing four layers of clothing as protection against my thin California blood.

By the time the manager approached the front door, key in hand, people were pounding on the door; it looked like a bakery during the French Revolution. They say heavy crowds operate under the law of fluid dynamics, and I believe it. This was like turning on the nozzle of a fire hose full blast.

A torrent of people flooded the store only held back by one closed door which eventually gave way. Naturally, all the cash registers were ready to rake in the take. We stationed people in the various aisles to answer questions and had a few items on super sale, for example a couple of beautiful down quilts were marked from $299 to $9.99. Now the secret of Black Friday which is forgotten from year to year is that the heavily marked down merchandise is in limited quantities, once we were out, we were out, and that is the source of more arguments and in some cases fist fights than any other element of this day of infamy.

One woman, who I shall kindly say was a bit portly, threw herself physically over the two quilts and refused to let an elderly lady near them.

Now these quilts were quite thick and it was difficult enough to wrap your arms around one. Normally, this lady would have retrieved a shopping cart, but that would have taken precious time, which was being measured as carefully as athletes in the Olympics.

So this woman struggled to take possession of both quilts while the elderly lady was enlisting help to get one away from her. She'd come with her grandson who looked as if he played for the New Mexico Lobos football team. He grabbed one quilt and summoning linebacker strength managed to free it from the first lady. She wasn't having any of that, though and with a mighty shove threw this mass of man into a display of King Size pillows, in which he became impossibly entangled.

"Nobody gets these fucking quilts but me," she shouted, drowning out Bing Crosby who was singing "Oh Little Town of Bethlehem" over the intercom. Like the filmmaker in "Fitzcaraldo" who manages to drag a boat up a waterfall, she pushed and pulled both quilts until the plastic covering shredded off so the product was picking up dirt and insect life from the floor of the store. She finally made it to a cash register and nearly passed out from the exertion. Slowly withdrawing a credit card she paid the tiny bill and then without thinking to put her purchase in a shopping cart, she schlepped both quilts across the parking lot and jammed them through the rear hatch of a Honda. They must have looked like hell and I can think of nobody who deserved two hellish looking quilts more than she.

The behavior throughout the store wasn't much better. It was "Mad Max" meets the Christmas spirit. The lines at the cash register seemed to stretch to infinity or at least as far as the eye could see. Most of the merchandise was not on some incredible, never to be duplicated sale price. This was a phenomenon of people who wanted to be first and get the best deal possible. One harried older man proclaimed, "I'll get a divorce before I let her put me through this again." I wonder if he did?

And Christmas season at J.C.Penney was just starting! The closer the big day came the more desperate the shoppers. Naturally we were running out of stock on a number of things, indigenous to the Home Store.

"Where can I find it?" Was the oft asked question.

My only answer was, "Our nearest Home Store is in El Paso."

I'm surprised I didn't get punched by some angry customer with only half a tank of gas left in the car and no budget for a fill-up. Once again I was struck by how little the retail madness had to do with the meaning of the holiday. Even though I'm not a Christian I can certainly appreciate what Christ's birth must mean to them. To sully it with behavior such as I've seen would certainly have angered the early Christians many of whom gave up their lives so their religion might survive. Today, I wonder if Christmas is more about keeping the economy going than whose birthday is being celebrated.

A chapter about J.C. Penney would be incomplete, however, without the phenomenon that begins the day after Christmas. Of course, I'm taking about returns. The store had a very liberal return policy, at least in part to protect the lives of its employees. I've always had the attitude that if I get a present that I really hate – which rarely happens – I give it to somebody else, or to a charity that benefits the poor. What I don't do is go back to the store and demand a refund on money I didn't spend.

I have this indelible image in my brain, however, that there are people who spend Christmas night accumulating everything they don't want to keep, rubbing their hands together in glee, and thinking – now here's a way to screw the system and put my hands on some serious jack.

At J.C. Penney they brought every conceivable type of merchandise back for a refund, in some cases, they returned things we didn't carry. One man insisted on $25 for a battery charger and even had the receipt from Sears to prove he bought it. Another woman swooped into the store demanding to see the manager. Under a plastic wrap was a genuine Balenciaga gown. Is there a person alive, with the money to afford a $3000 gown stupid enough to believe it was bought at J.C. Penney?

I tried to see the humor in all this, but standing on my feet for eight to ten hours a day was simply too much. I wasn't cut out for retail, and the experience brought home a conceit I had carried for too many years. I thought I could do just about anything that didn't require understanding long mathematical equations. Not true, I now realize that there are lots of jobs I could never perform well enough to keep from getting fired. It only gave me a greater appreciation of the people who do those jobs and I try to be nicer when I come across them. This was a part of my entire transition from a sort of Hollywood sperm to what my grandfather would have called a "mensch" (a real human being). Life's lessons often don't come easy, but this was particularly difficult. I've stopped looking down on people because of all the people who looked down on me, and probably still would if they could see my car or my disgusting apartment in the War Zone.

Although I had proven to myself I could earn a living, doing even what I had formerly considered menial work, there was still one more rock in the road that would increase my appreciation of what I had until I lost it.

CHAPTER THIRTY-NINE
We All Fall Down

On the Second of January, 2009 J.C. Penney let me go. There were people there that could do everything better than I, whether it was folding towels or stocking shelves.

When we parted company, the store manager said with a wry smile, "You didn't come this far in life by being great at retail. Why don't you go back to something you're really good at?"

Of course, he was right, but all my attempts to get back into television production had failed. I would keep trying but I had to find something to do in the meantime. Any thoughts as to what that something would be were ended when one day, while walking idly down the street, I tripped over something and fell head first to the sidewalk. Doing the natural thing, I threw out my arms to try and break my fall.

Awaiting me, at the exact level of my right wrist was a broken beer bottle. As I hit the bottle sliced deep inside my wrist and I began to bleed, badly. I ripped off my shirt and tried to make a tourniquet, but that only resulted in agony since there was glass in the wound. I started feeling woozy and reached for my phone and punched in 911.

"I've fallen on the street and slashed open my wrist, I feel like I'm going to pass out."

The operator kept me on the line, getting my location and keeping me conscious until the ambulance arrived. The pain was 11 on a scale of 10. It seemed like it took an hour for the ambulance to arrive, and longer still to get to the emergency room. They did x-rays of my wrist after injecting some sort of dye; my hand had gone numb and nobody would say a thing regarding when I might get my feeling back.

"You need to go to your primary care physician." The ER Doc told me.

"What about the numbness?" I asked with my heart in my throat.

"I don't know. Speak with your doctor and then plan what you will do," was all he would say.

Understand, I liked my doctor very much. She had a soft caring manner about her and always answered my questions. There is a tendency in patients to assume that every decision your doctor makes is the right one. That is a mistake as I was about to learn.

After examining the wound, checking the x-rays and tests, she told me I needed to wait six months to see if the severed nerves that were causing the numbness in my thumb, middle and ring fingers, would grow back and re-attach. If that happened there was no need for surgery, which she said did not always do the job.

"What about the pain?" I inquired.

"I don't like to give out narcotic pain relievers, but I'll give you one short prescription for Vicadin. After that you'll have to stick with ibuprofen. Besides, the pain is only temporary."

Wow, was she wrong. The pain was constant; it kept me up at night. All the things I had taken for granted such as unscrewing a jar or cutting my fingernails, were now impossible for me to do. I had no strength in my right hand, and even anything I tried to do with it was agonizing.

I waited four months and begged her for a referral to a hand surgeon. She sent me to a good one who was particularly honest. In his opinion I should have been sent to him immediately, now the only thing he could do was to attempt an operation which would, in layman's terms, blaze new pathways for the nerves to grow back and re-attach. Even then it was a 50-50 chance they wouldn't and I'd have to re-learn how to do everything that relied on a strong right hand.

The surgery lasted but a few hours and the medication that followed was Oxycodone, one step below morphine as I understand it. Very habit forming and hard on the stomach. It killed the post surgical pain, but left me woozy and a basket case. I was living alone and could hardly do anything for myself. I requested the pain killer be knocked down a notch and went back on Vicadin. Doing this meant I would have to learn to live with the pain, maybe it would get better. I taught myself how to do things that I had known all my life. Back in high school I took a class in typing. Considering how I've earned my living over the years it was the most purely useful class I ever took. At the time, my reason was less utilitarian. There were 29 girls in the class and I was the only boy.

Still I learned well and when computer keyboards came in I was ready for them. Now I had to re-learn to type using only three fingers on my right hand, and whereas in the past I could go on for hours, after ninety minutes the pain was bad enough that I had to stop and take something.

These are the conditions under which I wrote this book and anything else I write in the future, as the operation failed to restore normalcy to my right hand. I try hard not to wince when someone shakes my hand, I just hope they don't try to turn it into a squeezing contest. I still have to take painkillers, but there is a positive side effect. I've always had allergies that kept me with a stuffy nose. Apparently, Vicadin is a terrific anti-tussive that keeps me breathing more freely than I have ever experienced.

At the same time it became apparent that I could no longer work at any job that required any real strength in my right hand. I can type and take care of myself, but I had to give up just about any sport that didn't involve pushing a peanut with my nose. In addition, even when I sleep, I have to make sure my right hand is above my heart or the level of pain is simply unbearable.

Thankfully I could still have sex, now all I needed was a girlfriend, but even as life became more difficult and my chances of a comeback in my chosen profession became remote. With that thought I fell into a deep depression. All I wanted to do was sleep and that wasn't the solution to my many problems.

CHAPTER FORTY
A Midnight 911

If you've ever had a heart attack, then you know you live in fear. It doesn't matter how much medication you take, whether blood thinners, Lipitor, or Preparation H. There's always that thought in the back of your mind that it could happen again, and in the worst possible moment: on the freeway at 65 MPH. I know of at least one instance when that very thing happened.

I was seventeen and driving my Aunt Deenah's Ford Crown Victoria, a car with a mass only slightly less than a neutron star. We were going from her home in the valley to Zuma Beach, where all the "Vals" hung out. In the car were five of my cousins, including little two year old Geenah. We were stopped at the end of a traffic job on the Ventura Freeway, about two miles east of Malibu Canyon.

I looked in my rear view mirror and saw a horrifying sight. A car was bearing down on me and wasn't even slowing down. In the last fraction of a second before it hit, there was nothing I could do. I hit the brake as hard as I could and then suddenly everything went into slow motion. Seat belts were not installed in every car at that time and people were flying around the car hitting every obstruction. Somehow, Geenah went from the back seat to a position where she was stuck under front console. It would take an audio engineer to reproduce the sound of the impact as metal struck metal and all the cold equations went to work.

The car that hit us was a Corvair, a light rear engine car that Chevy made at the time. Ralph Nader wrote a book about them called "Unsafe at Any Speed." The driver of the Corvair struck his own windshield, which popped out of the car and flew 200 feet down the freeway. In the trunk of our Ford Crown Vic were two bowling balls – they were pulverized to dust.

Everyone in my Aunt's car wound up in the hospital. I was the least injured; my aunt sustained a fractured pelvis. The baby was hurt but recovered. The investigation into what became a multi car chain reaction accident showed the man in Corvair died of a heart attack with his foot depressing the accelerator. Thus I have reason to fear that scenario. Every time I look in my rear view mirror I wonder if it's going to happen again.

In fact, most heart attacks don't happen at 88 feet per second. Mine occurred while I was in bed, so every once in a while I find myself wondering if it will reoccur in the same way.

One night, shortly after leaving the J.C. Penney for the last time, I felt a pain in my chest. It was as though a hand was squeezing my heart, harder and harder. My breath was coming in short bursts and I was sweating profusely.

No, this couldn't be the end. I haven't made my come-back yet. Worse, there was no one around me to help. I grabbed my cell phone and hit 911. I crawled over to the door and unlocked it so they wouldn't have to break the lock and expose what little I had to the neighborhood thieves. With that I collapsed on the floor.

A few minutes later the door knob turned a paramedic in full kit pushed everything aside. He and his buddy were soon doing a blood pressure on me 160/125, lifting me onto a gurney, and taking me to the ER.

There was no waiting line for me at the ER, they pushed through everybody and before I knew it an IV line was in me and they were taking blood. When a heart attack occurs a certain protein is given off and that's what they look for in the lab. They hold you about eight hours and test you again since sometimes it takes that long for the protein to show up, and besides, they really don't want you conking on them.

The pressure in my chest was unabated and extremely painful. I was lying on an uncomfortable ER bed, lines running in and out of me, wishing I could go to sleep and awaken from this nightmare.

The ER Doc came in and spoke for a few minutes.

"Your record shows you had a Cabbage and a heart attack isn't very likely this soon after. Is there anything happening in your life that's causing you anxiety?" He asked.

"Well, I'm out of work, low on money, living in The War Zone and scared to death of having another heart attack, since I live alone and can't look to anyone for help."

The doctor shook his head, "That would be a source of high anxiety for anyone. Are you taking anything for it?"

"No just some anti-depressants that don't seem to have much effect."

"Okay, so far you're testing negative for a heart attack. Let's see if we can make you feel more comfortable."

With that he took out a syringe and emptied it into my IV.

"What is it?" I asked.

"It's a drug called Ativan, an anti-anxiolytic. It sounds like you're having a panic attack, whose symptoms can mirror a full scale coronary. Let's see how you feel in half an hour."

Sure enough in about twenty minutes the pain was gone and so was the anxiety. They kept me for another two hours and tested me once again, but it was negative. The doctor gave me a small prescription for Ativan and told me to see my doctor for more.

"By the way," he cautioned, "You don't want to stop taking this suddenly. The symptoms are pretty bad. It's called benzodiazepam withdrawal. When you no longer needed it let your doctor dial back the dosage gradually.

Great, another rock in the road. I'm taking a medicine I can't stop without special precautions.

They discharged me eight hours after the panic attack. I had to take a cab home to that grungy apartment, located in the Cocaine Corridor, where I was the only English speaking tenant.

It reminded me of a joke, an old friend named Mike Wiggins used to tell.

A guy is driving through the agricultural stretches of the great San Joaquin valley. He is totally lost, so he stops at a gas station outside Delano for directions. The attendant doesn't speak English, and "no comprendes" him as does the man at the cash register.

Frustrated, the driver looks to the sky and exalts, "Doesn't anybody around here speak English?"

To which the man replies, "English, we don't got to speak no stinking English. You're in Delano now."

Maybe I should learn Spanish.

CHAPTER FORTY-ONE
A Pebble in a Pond

It took five days for me to get an appointment with my cardiologist and my reward was a tortuous exam which included a walk till you drop treadmill test, with 32 electrical leads attached everywhere, except there. I failed to get my heart rate up to the figure the doctor requested and found myself exhausted and out of breath. You'd think I'd just run the "Ironman Triathlon."

Looking at the results of my test and especially my electrocardiogram, he had some shocking news for me.

"I'm afraid about 20% of your heart muscle is dead and will never regenerate."

"What does that mean, in real terms, doctor?" I asked.

"Well there are people living their lives with 50% of their heart muscle gone, but they have restrictions on what they can do and for how long they can do it. You can go on pretty much as normal, just don't over exert yourself and be aware that you could have another heart attack which would only make things worse."

"So I have one foot in the grave and the other on a banana peel?" Once again I tried to make light of a serious situation as the only way I could cope.

"I wouldn't say it's that bad, but whatever work you consider doing you have to realize that you are somewhat disabled."

Okay, so I was somewhat disabled, but not totally disabled. I could still write, produce and direct, as long as it didn't make any ridiculous physical demands on me. The question was: who was going to hire me under the circumstances. I mean, I couldn't find work in my profession when I was healthy.

I was distraught and depressed, but the next day I saw an ad on Craig's List for an experienced producer-director. I didn't waste anytime sending a cover letter and my five page list of credits and awards. I felt that I was on a mission and this could be my last chance to do what I was destined – or programmed – to do since childhood.

For the next week or so I answered every ad I could on Craig's List, most of which were for writing. I was amazed that most of the responses admitted to having no budget and I wasn't going to waste my valuable and limited energy doing a show for free. I was scared; I felt like every day could be my last.

Finally, I got a response from a man I'll simply call Dave. He was Executive Producing a project for a doctor who wanted to dramatize what a Board Certification Exam was like in various specialties. The pay wasn't great but it would allow me a few luxuries, like going out to dinner once in a while. So I agreed to meet with the guy who was really running the project, a well know anesthesiologist.

I liked the doctor, he was very sharp and planned to play one of the roles himself. We would do two scenarios initially. They would run 45 minutes and there would also be a promo, which he agreed to let me write. We got along well, but it was pretty apparent to me that his Executive Producer didn't know squat about television, or in this case, video production. I was going to have my hands full, for in addition to managing and directing the project, there was going to be a lot of handholding and explaining ahead.

But damn, I was back in business! The first thing I needed to do was find a production company, with cameras, lights, a green screen and people who knew what they were doing. I got lucky in that the first company I interviewed had it all. In my experience it takes dozens of interviews to find the right production company, especially one that matches my creative and artistic personality. Here in Albuquerque, a city immersed which Hollywood derogatorily refers to as "the fly-over" I found it on the first try. Even more important than a lot of abstract artistic sensibilities, I liked the people and felt they could do the heavy lifting, which was now beyond my capability.

Oh there were a few eccentricities but if you dare call yourself a producer, you know how to deal with them. The biggest one was that that doctor had built himself a make-shift studio in his backyard, it was really a converted barn, and wanted to shoot the scenarios there. As the medieval English song goes – translated into modern English – Summer is a cumin' in, and Albuquerque gets very hot, but like Las Vegas the humidity is low. I knew there would be a lot of sweating so we'd need copious amounts of make-up. In addition, we wouldn't be hiring actors, which is just as well. Actors would have a devil of a time getting through the medical terminology. If you've ever seen an episode of "House" you know docs can sling a lot of multisyllabic words around. Well this involved 2, 45 minute scenarios that were all multi-syllabic, no scenes, just questions, answers and more questions. It was "House" on steroids, the equivalent of making a motion picture in a language you don't understand and your staff can't translate.

To demonstrate the pressure doctors come under during these exams, the questions were fired rat-a-tat-tat, like words coming out of a machine gun. Sometimes the answers were cut off with the examiners making rude remarks, designed to throw the examinees off stride, to see if they could cope with pressure.

At first Dave expected the doctor/actors were going to memorize everything, mostly because he didn't want to spend the money on a teleprompter. I explained that it was an impossible expectation and I simply wasn't going to do it without a prompter and skilled operator. The teleprompter fits under the camera and scrolls the dialog so the doctor/actor simply has to read. It's not as easy as it sounds even for people who read prompters for a living. To stay within budget they wanted to do the entire shoot in a single day.

To give you an idea how crazy that is, on a movie if you do four pages a day that's considered good work. We were going to do 75 pages in one day. Due to the availability of the actor/doctors and the constraints of the studio, we had to shoot the questioners separately from the examinee, which means we had to cue every line of dialog.

Normally, I would have thrown down the gauntlet and said, "No," but I had to establish some sort of reputation in Albuquerque and basically show I could do the impossible. At this point I should say humbly that without Brian Buckley and Ben Harrison it truly would have been impossible.

The day of the shoot dawned and it was hot. I had nervous actor/doctors – fish out of water – all over the place. It was time to remove my producing hat and don my director's chapeau, which happens to be a "good luck" hat I had worn at a World Series game that the Dodgers won.

The temperature inside the studio was over 120F and we periodically had to stop shooting, shut down the lights, open the door and let it cool down to 95F, while our talent was getting fresh make up applied. There were times I thought we'd never make it, but after a very hard eleven hours, we shot our last frame against the green screen background. We would later shoot inside a hotel room to provide a proper setting, the type of room in which these horrific exams were actually conducted. Most important, my boss the doctor praised my leadership – of all the things a director must be, he or she must be a leader, through thick and thin, food breaks, multiple takes, and equipment failure. When things go wrong everybody looks to the director to put it right; that is where I wanted to be and certainly was on this day.

As principal photography came to an end, I was congratulated on a job well done under the most difficult conditions. At that moment I was flying. I was doing the one thing I really knew how to do. Something you don't learn at J.C. Penney's.

Now all we had to do was cut it all together and make it look good and that took over a month. If you've never been in a edit bay with its overwhelming compliment of equipment and language that is as arcane as the med-speak of the doctors, you'll either be fascinated or bored to death. Fortunately, I eat up every minute in editing, because you can often take a scene which isn't playing and make it work. I've spent a third of my adult life in this setting, and if I had to choose a place to take my last breath, it would be laying the final frame of the final film and calling a wrap.

My editing experience goes way back before the days of the modern non-linear editing systems, to equipment that took as many as five computers to operate and rented for $500 an hour. If you didn't know what you were doing, and had the wrong equipment listed for your job, you could easily run up a $20,000 bill and not accomplish anything. Fortunately, three decades of experience makes that less likely.

So, after six weeks of post production we finally delivered the edit masters to the doc. Dave, who frustrated me so much had long since disappeared from the production. It seems he was a thorn in more sides than mine.

At that point you might ask what do you do? Well, not wanting to disappoint anybody, but there was no million dollar wrap party, I didn't go out and get plastered. There was simply a few questions on my mind, now that I reassured myself that I could earn a living, doing my thing, but what was I going to do next, and what after that.

Fortunately, the answers were not long in coming.

CHAPTER FORTY-TWO
Gold Strike

Having finished the videos for the Doctor's On-Line Board Reviews I was anxious not to lose momentum. I could feel the old creativity returning after much too long a hiatus. What could I do now?

I have had a life long flirtation with the sport of bowling. Now there are some who contend it's more of a past time, but those who do, have no idea of how difficult it is bowl consistently good. I've known people who have bowled for years, even decades and never averaged over 150.

I was introduced to the game at a birthday party when I was ten. We bowled at the now defunct Pan Pacific Bowl, which was so backward they still used pin boys. Naturally, I wasn't very good, but something about the game got to me. I started watching television shows like Championship Bowling and Bowling Stars and soon had a retinue of favorite professional bowlers. When I turned 11 my biggest birthday present was a Brunswick Black Beauty bowling ball, the make and model used by Don Carter, who at that time was probably the best bowler in the world.

With a new ball, I started bowling junior leagues, improved a lot, and soon I was winning trophies for bowling over 200. Today that doesn't seem like a big deal, but the game has changed over the years. All we had were hard rubber bowling balls and the lanes were covered by a type of lacquer. Today, the balls are made of exotic materials and the lanes use patterned oil, which can make it easy or impossibly difficult to score.

At any rate, I bowled in leagues for about twenty years, and then as my work got more intense I became a sporadic bowler. I would try and practice at times when the centers weren't crowded and the lanes were pretty fresh. I remember on one occasion, being the only person at Wagon Wheel Bowl in Oxnard, and shooting 17 strikes in 19 frames. It got the attention of the guy behind the desk, who wanted to know if I was a pro.

When Torrey came along, I decided to spend more time with her, and didn't bowl much at all with one exception. I did a lot of editing at a post production house in North Hollywood called Premore. It seems they were entering a bowling team in a charity tournament sponsored by the Motion Picture Association of America. The general manager of Premore, Bob Perry, a good friend, asked me if I would bowl for his team as a ringer. I agreed and managed to bowl high game and high series (I think it was 728 for three games – not bad for an amateur at the time) and the team finished second. That was fun, but there were other things in my life and on my plate and the active side of the game just slipped away.

I'd always wanted to do a bowling show, but the only major program on television dedicated to the sport was the PBA (Professional Bowler's Association) tournaments on ESPN. In 1960, I was at Hollywood Legion Lanes in the audience of Jackpot Bowling, inexplicably hosted by Milton Berle, when Therm Gibson won $60,000 by getting six strikes in a row. That was giant money at the time. What if I could award big money to an amateur for shooting a single strike?

Too easy, almost anyone can get a strike, although it's made more difficult being on television under the lights, but to award big money how could I make it really difficult? As I mentioned earlier, contemporary bowling is about "playing the oil," the pattern of dressing laid down on the lane, to keep it from being destroyed by all the bowling balls hitting it. Amateurs and league bowlers typically bowl on what's called a "house pattern," a standardized way of putting down the oil that makes it relatively easy to score. After all, what would you rather shoot 140 or 190? If you put pros on that same condition they'll shoot 240 and a lot of 300's. It's much too easy. So the PBA came up with all kinds of tricky patterns to make it more difficult to consistently put the ball between the one and three pins (one and two if you're a lefty). Their patterns have all kinds of names like shark and chameleon; I had to find the toughest oil pattern in existence to put my amateurs on but only for the big money shot.

So I came up with a format. Eight bowlers would start. They'd bowl on a regular house condition, bowling one on one single frame matches until they eliminated down to four, then two and finally one would remain. The last one standing would get one shot on what became the Gold Strike lane (with gold pins to accent). That particular lane wouldn't be bowled on until the big shot – at $50,000! Thus I was taking an amateur, putting them under the pressure on television and the oil pattern I finally decided upon was identical to the one the pros shot on in the U.S. Open. It's the hardest pattern to hit, and you have to be really good to get a strike. That reduced the odds of a strike from one in two or one in three to about one in thirty. If only one show out of every thirty gave away the top prize, I could afford to make this work financially.

Brian Buckley, my co-producer and Ben Harrison, my art director and editor came up with ideas of their own. We'd have a wacky cam sequence, with somebody doing something really stupid on the lanes. Then there would be a little bowling quiz, another element to keep the show moving. It was up to me to come up with something big and I was lucky enough to talk one of the finest women bowlers in the world, Missy Bellinder, to come on the show and give advice to the person who would make the big shot.

So we had the elements together for a pilot show which would be used to sell the concept and have a copyrightable program. On October 11, 2009 I put on my director's hat while others worked tirelessly to transform ten lanes of Gary Skidmore's Holiday Bowl into a big set with two lanes for general competition and a Gold Strike lane for the big money. There was just one problem, I had to get the bowlers and the audience to act as though they were really bowling for $50,000. We were financing the pilot ourselves and didn't have that kind of money to give away.

I put on another hat and warmed up the audience. I had seen Ed McMahon do warm ups for "TV's Bloopers and Practical Jokes" and "The Tonight Show." A warm up is to get the audience in the mood so they'll laugh, cheer and applaud at the appropriate moments. You do it by making them part of the production. Their reaction is important to whether the show will succeed or fail. Most people are good sports and go along.

Before we started taping I went in front of our assembled audience who we'd put on bleachers laid down on lane one and did my thing. They laughed and cheered; they were positively wonderful and it shows when you watch the pilot show.

A week before we had selected eight bowlers from the locals, they ranged from 20-60 in age and had a wide variety of bowling talent. I revved them up and told them that the winner would get a chance to really bowl for $50,000 if we sold the show. They did quite a job. There were a lot of strikes and several matches went into a "bowl off" the equivalent of sudden death overtime.

Finally, it came down to a very cute young woman who happened to tend bar at the bowling center. She had eliminated everybody including a guy, who definitely didn't want to lose to a girl, but that's the way the pins fall.

Missy came out and to show that a strike was possible, blasted a high flush which put every pin in the pit (though it took her two attempts – the miss we edited out of the show). She told Amanda (our finalist) what she need to do to get a strike. Trust me, Amanda had never bowled on a US Open lane condition, she came close but went high on the head pin leaving a split.

We couldn't let her go home with nothing, so we presented her with a gift certificate from Albertson's Supermarket for $35 that Brian had inveigled from a store manager. The live taping was finished. We had shot in high definition with six cameras and now had a lot of tape to edit down into a 22 minute show.

Ben designed some state-of-the-art graphics and then we went into editing. I've always known that I was probably at my happiest in the edit bay. Producers, Directors and Editors speak their own language, which is highly technical and incomprehensible to anyone who has never done it – what we call a civilian. It took the better part of three weeks because there were some problems with the audio, a lot of which had to be replaced and then edited back into synchronization through a process called ADR (Automated Dialog Replacement). It was tricky, but in the end we had a show that frankly was more fun than I would have imagined. In the process I was having the time of my life, harkening back to the days I spent in the edit bay working for Dick Clark, Johnny Carson and on my own videos for the home market.

This was me, the guy that nearly died three times, who lost his family, his home and all the money he'd accumulated in a lifetime; a man who became homeless, sick, went through horrific surgeries, lived in the worst neighborhood in Albuquerque, did relatively menial jobs, and finally made it back to do what he was born to do.

At the first screening of the Gold Strike pilot I sat back in the chair and thought, "My God, Donald, where have you been?"

CHAPTER FORTY-THREE
A New Home

Funny how timing is everything. When you least expect it, your whole world comes crashing down, then when no one is looking something good can actually happen.

December 31, 2009 – New Years Eve was absolutely the last straw for me living in the war zone. There is something of an Hispanic tradition about firing off a single shot to welcome in the new year at midnight. That has always scared the hell out of me because any bullet that's shot up in the air has to come down somewhere. You'd have thought the tradition makers would have considered that little bit of elementary physics, but it didn't and neither did all the people who feel compelled to follow the it.

Anyway, this alone keeps me from going out on New Year's Eve in Albuquerque. I mean who wants to go celebrate the arrival of a new year and wind up dead one minute after midnight. So I stayed up late for two reasons. One, was I wanted to see how Dick Clark looked for his brief appearance on television. Remember, I worked for the guy and became rather fond of him and his family. The other reason was that the gunfire would wake me up anyway. So I'm watching ABC-TV waiting for the ball drop in Times Square and then as the ball got half way down it started. It wasn't an isolated shot here and there, but fusillades of shots coming from every possible direction. I scrambled trying to get under the kitchen table and then I heard someone unload an entire clip from a fully automatic weapon and it sounded right outside my window.

My first thought was someone's got an AK-47 with a banana clip, quickly followed by oh shit all those bullets one of them might have my name written on it. By 12:01 the world outside sounded like Saigon during the Tet offensive.

I gotta get an Ativan, no that's stupid, I'll just be more relaxed when they find my bullet riddled body. This was the last straw. As the old song went, "I just had to get out of this place." The problem was I was out of work and out of money, the car dealer was dinging me for a payment and my food stamps had run out. You don't get any broker than that.

Then the next day, I get a call from Shannon, thinking it's just a New Year's wish.

"Hi Don, did you see in the paper that someone in your neighborhood got killed by a stray bullet last night?"

"You're kidding! Only one!"

"We've got to find you another place to live and I mean right away." She said emphatically.

"Bless you Shannon, but I'm somewhat financially embarrassed right now."

"Never you mind, I'm putting my friend on the project. He'll find you something."

"Thanks, I don't think I could survive another year here, with or without the gunfire."

A bit later Shannon got back to me. Low cost, decent housing simply wasn't in long supply, but she had done a lot of looking. It turns out that Damon was working two jobs, one for the New Mexico Business Weekly and the other managing a beautiful apartment/condo complex. Initially I was skeptical, but I couldn't remain where I was and maintain any degree of sanity, so one Sunday morning – when it was safe to go out – I drove across the Rio Grande to the west side of town and followed the directions to the complex.

It was everything Shannon had said and more. Enough space for my needs, clean as whistle, beautifully landscaped, and in a decent neighborhood. It was close to everything and the rent was very reasonable. Keep in mind that since leaving J.C. Penney I hadn't made all that much money.

First I had to fill out a stack of forms that wanted to know everything about my life, my health, my net worth (ha what a joke), and after a few screenings I got the place. A whole team of friends helped me move in. At last I have a place to live where I feel safe and can actually invite people over. Everybody remarks on what a nice complex it is, and how much they like the place, which Shannon nicknamed "The Condominiam." That surely is at least a beginning for the rest of my life.

CHAPTER FORTY-FOUR
This is the Day Kid

January 19, 2010 – What a day! A month ago I was contacted by a prominent Albuquerque attorney named Daniel J. Macke. I wasn't expecting an attorney to call me and at first there was a little apprehension. Was Jackie suing me or what? Perhaps he wanted to make a television show.

As it turns out I had a surprise in store for me, a pleasant one at that. Dan was Co-Chairman of the Board at the Albuquerque Opportunity Center. He wanted to know if I would join the Board of Directors. It sounded like he was prepared to do a sell job, but it wasn't necessary. What an honor for me! We had lunch shortly afterward to discuss what I could do for AOC, which is part of the Metropolitan Homelessness Project.

Having been homeless, I told him I would do whatever I could to help them whether it meant doing some pro bono video work or helping to raise money through my talent as a public speaker. Hey these people saved my life, why wouldn't I want to show my appreciation? I began immediately thinking about what I could do, what contribution I could make to end homelessness forever.

Today, at the noon meeting of the Board, I'm to be elected. Daniel will introduce me and then (unlike politics) it's a done deal. Look at what's happened to me in a relatively short few years.

I first walked in the door of the Albuquerque Opportunity Center as a homeless man with virtually nothing but a few meager possession, the clothes on my back, without much hope or belief in the future. My very mettle was tested by one trauma after another. How many times I wanted to give up, to let my life flow down and down until I was unrecognizable even to myself.

All those times I went to bed not knowing if I would awaken the next morning. I had known despair greater than I would have thought possible. Something kept me going. Maybe it was just surviving from day to day, but I'd been inspired along the way and befriended by wonderful people. How many of us, in our lifetime lose an entire family and then find our way into another. God bless Bren and Shannon for taking me into their world, making me feel like blood kin. Then there were the wonderful friends I had made in a city where I was a complete stranger. Now I was going to join a group that consisted of people I really admired. The other co-chairman is the Reverend Trey Hammond, a man who through his life and work had done so much to help the homeless that I can't even begin to recount it all. Besides, knowing him, he's probably a little embarrassed even to be mentioned.

Then there's Dennis Plummer who is the Executive Director, the top guy on the line at AOC. Others like, David Cisneros and Jessica Casey(I'm sorry for not naming everyone) who give tirelessly in their efforts to help not just the homeless, but the people who have taken ill and have no place to go; veterans who returned from the hell of war in the Middle East and for whatever reasons found themselves on the streets. My fellow board members are without exception amazing folks, who work on often without the recognition they deserve (I hope this helps a little).

The past three years have changed me forever. I am not the person I was before the singularity that ended one life and began another. My journey has taken me not just miles, but light years in terms of how I view the world and myself.

My Uncle Walter always talked about humility although I can't recall ever seeing him display it. Well, I found it by become the least member of society and working my way back to where I could take a little personal pride in my accomplishments. I no longer view the world through a pair of Hollywood glasses, at the same time I've been given a rare opportunity to really help people, so that when my last day finally comes, I'll know why I was here.

Yes, this is the day, kid—you've learned the hard way that although it feels like nobody knows you when you're down and out, in fact people care enough to extend a helping hand. It took a lot good human beings but you've endured some of the worst trials a person can face. You have survived and endured your own personal purgatory and here you are at the Harwood Methodist Church to attend a meeting which will elevate you in your eyes, and possibly the eyes of a few good friends.

Now what will I do with this opportunity? Well as of now the fist thing will be to periodically visit the men in respite care and listen to what they have to say. Do everything I can to help them survive this time in their lives.

Then in the coming months I want to make a documentary, that chronicles homelessness through the eyes of the homeless; give the rest of society a look at their world and perhaps, just maybe, some percentage of those who view it will want to help. Perhaps they'll make a donation to a local homeless charity or one of the big national charities like the United Way. Maybe a few will volunteer to work in their hometown shelters, to talk to people who they didn't feel they had much in common, but we all share the same basic chemistry, not to mention hopes and dreams.

Speaking of dreams, I'd like to see an end to this situation in the United States of America. I want care for people who have mental illness they didn't ask for, they deserve treatment not derision. Even people who are substance abusers, drug addicts to put it bluntly need our help to reclaim their own lives. I don't look down on them, because in another set of circumstances there go I.

Ultimately I'm writing these memoirs, as difficult as it has been reliving a time the old "me" would have preferred to forget in the hope that I can shed a little bit of light on what can happen to an ordinary person in this life and more importantly the meaning of redemption. I had to die, three times, before I found my soul. This is a day like no other. I wanted to share it with you, because I have to.

6

LaVergne, TN USA
04 February 2011
215180LV00003B/1/P